*

things no one will tell fat girls

things
NO ONE
will tell
FAT
girls

A Handbook for Unapologetic Living

JES BAKER

SEAL PRESS

Things No One Will Tell Fat Girls
Copyright © 2015 Jes M. Baker

Seal Press
A Member of the Perseus Books Group
1700 Fourth Street
Berkeley, California
sealpress.com

Library of Congress Cataloging-in-Publication Data

Baker, Jes.
Things no one will tell fat girls / by Jes Baker.
pages cm

ISBN 978-1-58005-582-6 (paperback)
1. Overweight women--Psychological aspects. 2. Body image in women. 3. Self-esteem in women. 4. Self-care, Health. I. Title.
RC628.B28 2015
613'.04244--dc23
2015019704

10 9 8 7 6 5 4 3 2

Cover design by Faceout Studios, Kara Davison
Interior design by Domini Dragoone
Printed in the United States of America
Distributed by Publishers Group West

For all the fat girls

who have no idea that

*they are **absolutely** perfect*

contents

INTRODUCTION 1

ONE
What in the World Is Body Love, and Why Does It Matter? 9

TWO
Start Now, GODDAMNIT: Waiting Doesn't Work 18

guest essay: Virgie Tovar 25

THREE
You Hate Your Body Because Don Draper Told You To:
Throw Some Shade at History 28

guest essay: Sonya Renee Taylor 43

FOUR
If You're Happy and You Know It, Cut in Line:
Fat Hate Isn't Your Problem 47

guest essay: Andrew Walen 61

FIVE
Fat and Health: Rethink That Shit 64

guest essay: Jen McLellan 82

SIX
Selfies Aren't Selfish: Narcissism Is Good for You 86

SEVEN
Change Your Tumblr, Change Your Life:
Diversify Your Media Feed **105**

guest essay: Shanna Katz Kattari **116**

EIGHT
100% of Humans Have Brains:
Mental Health Support Is for Everyone **121**

guest essay: Kimberly A. Peace, MSW **140**

NINE
Watch Your Language: Words Matter **144**

guest essay: Sam Dylan Finch **166**

TEN
"Fatshion" Is a Form of Political Resistance:
Wear What Scares You **170**

guest essay: Bruce Sturgell **187**

ELEVEN
Affirmations Aren't Just for People Who Love Sedona:
You Can Rewire Your Brain **190**

TWELVE
Fat Girls Find Love Too: Yes, That Includes You **197**

guest essay: Chrystal Bougon **213**

THIRTEEN
Loving Your Body Will Change the World **217**

Resources **223**
Notes **232**
Acknowledgments **241**

*

introduction

I was really hoping that by the end of the writing process, my editor would have suggested some really clever way to open this book since I'm at a complete loss as to how to do this myself. But alas, no cigar. So you're stuck with me, and this is what I came up with: Hey there! I'm Jes Baker and if you've heard of me, I'm really glad you're here. And if you haven't heard of me? That's cool, too. Given that you just picked up a book with the words "fat" and "unapologetic" (two of my favorites), there's a good chance that this could be the start of a beautiful new friendship.

Yep. That's all I got.

After that informationless opening you might be wondering if this book is for you, and I want to save you time, so lemme break it down for ya: if you are a person who has spent your entire life feeling horrible about your body and you think that self-hatred kinda sucks, this book is for you. If you're interested in this totally bizarre concept called body love that you keep hearing about on *Upworthy* and *BuzzFeed* and you wanna know what it's all about, this book is for you. If you're intimidated by academic texts but still want to have a conversation about body acceptance, this book is for you. If you feel the need to hold something that says you're a valuable person (just as you are, right now) and reading websites just doesn't cut it, this book is for you. If you need a refresher course on why loving your body is not only possible, but critical, this book is for you. If you're a "fat" chick (who might be scared of that word) and you're convinced that your body is bad and holding you back from living an amazing life, this book is for you. If you're looking for a book that might offend your sensitivities at some point and has more italicized and capitalized words than you know what to do with . . . this book is *SO* for you.

If you are a *person* with a *body* who is tired of being shamed and told to shape up, slim down, camouflage, alter against your will, or make apologies for your body . . . THIS BOOK IS FOR YOU.

If you're still here, welcome. I've got a lot of important shit to share with you. But first, a few things about me, because we've established that we're about to become friends, after all.

Things you can find if you Google me:

1. I write a blog called *The Militant Baker*, and it's about body image, feminism, "fatshion," and mental health.

2. I wore badass saddle shoes when I was six.

3. I did a really famous photo campaign and challenged Abercrombie & Fitch's CEO to do a shirtless photo shoot with a fat chick. (Yep, I did that. He never responded, but he expressed that he was sorry he said rude things about fat girls, and to now make up for it the company will take your money if you want them to. See Chapter 10 for more dirty details.)

4. I have three cats and I love them more than almost anything.

5. I swear. A LOT.

6. I founded a conference once, for body love discussions to happen IRL (in real life).

7. I'm fat.

Things that actually matter here and now:

7. I'm fat.

No really, that's the most important thing.

Yes, I am also intelligent, snarky, kind, radical, compassionate, self-starting, outgoing, funny, opinionated, cheerful, loud, and a million other things. But here and now, I want to talk about the thing that strangers see first, the thing that I'm judged on the most. The reason I'm here writing this book right now: I'm pretty damn fat.

I know what you're thinking. *But Jes, don't call yourself fat! You're just chubby. Fluffy. Curvy. Chunky. Plus-size.* (Insert additional euphemisms here.)

Naw girl, I'm Fat.

Here's why I use the "f-word" ALL THE TIME: the word "fat" is not inherently bad. It's an adjective. It's a benign descriptor of size. As Marianne Kirby explains, "'Fat' means adipose tissue. 'Fat' means 'having a lot of adipose tissue.' There are no other words that mean precisely those things in precisely those ways."[1] Saying "I'm fat" is (and should be) the same as saying my shoes are black, the clouds are fluffy, and Bob Saget is tall. It's not good, it's not bad, it just is. The only negativity that this word carries is that which has been socially constructed around it; our aversion is completely learned. It's our association that is disparaging, and *this* is what we must change. We don't need to stop using the word "fat," we need to stop the hatred that our world connects with the word "fat." So I use it (often—you'll read it over 370 times in this book), because I have decided that it's *my* word now. And the more I use it positively, the more stigma I smash.

Now, I don't ever walk up to strangers and say "Hey Fatty!" Because, we haven't found a way to normalize it in the mainstream, there is a *really* good chance that the word is still offensive to them. But me calling *myself* fat? Ain't no thang. I even find the word empowering. Someone tries to insult me by calling me "fat"? I just say, "Yep. And?"

I have a fat body, and I think it's quite lovely.

But because our society still thinks that fat bodies are especially vile, I'm automatically put into several kinds of "boxes." Boxes with darling labels like *cultural deviant*—a freak of physical nature. Or *embarrassment to society*—when strangers or extended family moan and groan about the *horrific obesity crisis* in America? Yeah, they are talking about me. I'm also *your worst nightmare*. I'm the reason you diet. I'm the reason you go to the gym. I'm your "thinspiration" . . . because, god knows, you do *not* want to end up like me.

If you're fat too, you probably know what I'm talking about.

A few years ago I decided I would no longer accept these negative labels. After a breakup for which my body was blamed, I found myself at a critical impasse, a metaphorical fork in the road. I knew that I needed to carefully choose, right then and there, which path I was going to take: continue to hate my body, or learn to *love* my body.

It really was that black and white. I wasn't (and still am not) going to lose 110 pounds overnight and suddenly be "okay." So I made the best decision of my life: I decided to love my body. And then I decided to write about it online. These decisions instigated a transformation for me and (as a result) for the millions of people that have read the ridiculous shit I post. Since then, I've become completely enveloped in the world of body activism, and, as it turns out . . . that world is one I very much need.

The Militant Baker was not my first attempt at blogging. A year before that, I was posting weekly under a page titled *The Kitschen*. A small, vintage-inspired "lifestyle blog," nothing special, nothing new, one in a sea of similar concepts. This trite blog may have been insignificant in terms of its content, but it led me into the world of blogging, and eventually, to a discovery that changed everything.

Long before making the radical decision to love my body, I often spent nights tirelessly blog hopping, following one sidebar recommendation after another, enjoying the polished images and content that reminded me of magazines, only *way* cooler. I will never forget the night that I stumbled across *The Nearsighted Owl*, written by Rachele. This blog baffled me. It had all the components I loved—recipes, owls, polka dots, and purple beehives—but with one difference. Rachele was fat. She was not *only* fat: She was fat, confident, and *happy*. How. The. Fuck. Does. That. Happen? Scrolling through her posts, my mind was momentarily broken, trying to wrap itself around the fact that there was a woman in the world who looked nothing like the "ideal," but who was living a full and joyous life. No shame, no apologies, only confident posts about her favorite books, her art projects, her marriage (this is where I discovered that fat people get married too!), and her heroes. I continued to visit the page out of genuine curiosity, and soon I was hit with the most revolutionary thought: Maybe I don't have to loathe myself for the rest of my life.

Maybe I don't have to loathe myself for the rest of my life!

Maybe I can even sort of . . . like myself! Could it be true?!? Well, if Rachele can do it, perhaps . . . yeah. Maybe I can too! It's astounding to me that I hadn't realized this before. But, fuck. I'm glad that I did at age 26. Better late than never, right?

After discovering Rachele, I dove headfirst into the body positive community. I sought out photos of all kinds of women, I followed progressive Tumblr accounts, and I read every fat acceptance book I could get my chubby hands on. I read all the body love blogs I could find, researched the history of body image, and started to talk about all of this with people around me.

As I learned more about body love, I started to notice something interesting: The way I perceived the world shifted considerably. I quickly became less judgmental, not only of others, but also of myself! I was reformatting my reality. I was rewiring my belief in beauty. I was teaching myself the truth.

I also started to realize perfection isn't always what it seems in other areas of life, either. In a pivotal article I read in *Bitch* Magazine, called "Better Homes and Bloggers," Holly Hilgenberg calls out lifestyle blogs and how they tend to gloss over domestic life, often portraying a perfected world that's very different from reality.[2] Seeing depictions of this unrealistic world in a medium like blogging—that we tend to consider more realistic than other media—Hilgenberg notes, is damaging to readers who see these perfect families, homes, and art projects and think, "Jesus H. Christ, why isn't *my* life like that?" Hilgenberg compares these websites to photoshopped images in magazines and asks how helpful and different from magazines and television these blogs really are. When I read that, I thought . . . *well, fuck. I'm gonna create something representational of real life.*

And then I did.

I transitioned *The Kitschen* to *The Militant Baker*, which debuted as an honest (and poorly written) look at my life. It was "amateur hour" for at *least* a year when I started that blog, but I stuck to my guns and portrayed my real life. While other bloggers were publishing "a-photo-an-hour" posts and displaying pictures of their kitschy mug of coffee next to their cat bathing in the sun snuggled against their new cross-stitch projects, I was posting pictures of my sink full of dirty dishes and my shampoo mohawk creations in the shower. I wrote about tough topics like self-care, nighttime depression, emotional "first aid kits," and why leaving the house without makeup was radical. I made a point to write about the things that were raw and relevant in my very imperfect life.

To be clear: There's nothing *wrong* with writing about Samsonite luggage and vinyl records, but the obvious contrast between my blog posts and others' made me feel like I was saying what needed to be said while also getting away with something. And I loved it. The ability to be down-and-dirty honest in the digital world of sparkling houses and perfect "Friendsgivings" was intoxicating. I loved the thrill of reckless transparency. Fortunately, that thrill has never faded.

As I explored the concept of body acceptance, it started to overtake my thoughts, actions, and consequently, my blog. I started participating in body love challenges, posting full-body pictures with my dress size showing loud and proud on the images. I started writing about painful memories in posts like "Mental Souvenirs from the Life of a Fat Girl." I started to reclaim the word "fat," using it with carefree abandon and reveling in the fact that I was getting away with loving myself just as I was. My journey toward loving all of me (appearance included) started to take over, and I was thrilled to have such liberating content to share. *The Militant Baker* quickly became the body positive blog it's known as today.

As I continued to read, write, and research over the last few years, I began to realize that my entire life up until that point had been spent listening to *do*'s and *do not*'s created by selfish, money-lovin' companies and reinforced by people who believed them. They created and then sold the concept that conforming and constantly trying to change your body to become "better" was an applaudable life goal. It seems ridiculous to me now, but we've all believed those same companies and people at some point in our lives. It took me a while, but eventually I found the nerve to say NO MORE, MOTHERFUCKERS!, and I started to actually live life according to a *new* rule I made up, which basically went like this: RULES ARE FOR CHUMPS AND I'M GONNA DO WHATEVER THE FUCK I WANT. That non-rule "rule" led to so many epiphanies and revelations that a blog started to seem insufficient, and I realized I needed a book to contain them all. *This* is that book.

So, why is the fact that I'm fat the most important thing for you to know about me? Well, because as far as body shapes go, it's the most reviled in our society. Because my journey toward learning to love a body that I have been told is unworthy has been life changing. Because learning to love my body as it is has convinced me that not only is it possible, but it's necessary to living a truly happy and fulfilling life. Because I want you to have the opportunity to hear these revelations too. Because being fat and learning how to accept it has defined my mission as a body activist.

So, WELCOME.

You may think this is just another self-help book penned by

another smart-aleck chick with another inspirational message (and you'd be right), but it's more than that.

 This is also a compilation of the shit no one talks about. A collection of the hardest lessons I've ever learned. A literary homage to my triumph over shame, self-harm, depression, guilt, and self-sabotage. This is what the sound of the "Hallelujah Chorus" would look like if we were forced to see it through little letters on a page. This is a book about things that I wish I knew earlier. Things I've learned in real life. Things people really need to talk about more. This is a book full of things no one will ever tell fat girls . . . but shit. I will.

 So hold onto your knickers, y'all. Because if you play your cards right, this book could change your goddamn life.

*

what in the world is body love, and why does it matter?

[CHAPTER ONE]

If you're wondering why the hell I would take the time to write an entire book about things no one will tell people about their bodies, you're not the only one. And if you're skeptical about the fact that I place so much focus on something as seemingly vapid as our appearance, you're not alone.

People ask me all the time, "Why are you so superficial, Jes'ca?!? Why isn't your focus on inner beauty? Why aren't we talking about what we contribute to the world? Why aren't we discussing how marvelous our souls are?"

My personal conclusion goes something like this: We are more likely to be told by the world that we are good people than anything else. Funny, creative, intelligent, communicative, generous, maybe even extraordinary. What we are *not* told is that our bodies are perfect just the way they are. Like, ever. We are taught that our outsides are flawed, and not only that, but the majority of our worth lies in our physical appearance, which, of course is never "good enough" according to our society. They love to show us examples of unattainable physical perfection while demanding that we become the impossible, and because of this our bodies and our relationship to our bodies affect everything else in our lives on a monumental level.

We become too embarrassed to meet up with the friend we haven't seen in years because we might have gained weight. We sabotage relationships by thinking we're unworthy of physical affection. We hide our face when we have breakouts. We opt out of the dance class because we're worried we'll look ridiculous. We miss out on sex positions because we're afraid we'll crush our partner with our weight. We dread family holidays because someone might say *something* about how we look. We don't approach potential friends or lovers because we assume they will immediately judge our appearance negatively. We try to shrink when walking in public spaces in order to take up as little room as possible. We build our lives around the belief that we are undeserving of attention, love, and amazing opportunities, when in reality this couldn't be further from the truth.

Our bodies are installation art that we curate publicly. Our bodies are the first message those around us receive. Our bodies are our physical bookmarks that hold space for us in the world. Our bodies are magnificent houses for everything else that we are. Our bodies are a part of us, just as our kindness, talents, and passion are a part of us. Yes, we are so much more than our outer shells, but our outer shells are an integral part of our being, too. *This* is why I focus on them. **The way we view our bodies impacts the way we participate in the world** . . . and wouldn't it be wonderful if we could lose the bullshit we're taught and love our bodies for the perfect things that they are?

I just read a really great article in *Bitch* Magazine called "Pretty Unnecessary" where Lindsay King-Miller rightfully questions the focus on the importance of beauty within the body positive movement. She says, "While I'm in favor of encouraging women to feel confident and happy, I worry that today's body positivity focuses too much on

THE
**FAT
PEOPLE:**
do all the things!
CHALLENGE
*

Look for these challenges throughout the book, drawn from my satirical blog post series, "25 Things Fat People Shouldn't Do." All the items on this list come from ridiculous corners of the Internet where apparent "experts" have decided what fat people should and should not do. They range from the absurd to the profoundly shameful, from ridiculous things like doing a cannonball to making art. To this I said: *"Fuck that noise!* I'm doing them anyway." I "broke" every single one. But know this: If your size makes you feel too uncomfortable to do some of these challenges, that's okay! You do not need to actually *do them* to know that you're allowed to live a full life just like everyone else. However, if you *want* to give the middle finger to the part of society that says fat bodies aren't allowed to participate in certain activities, you're more than welcome to. All of this is your choice. That's the point here: You can and deserve to do whatever makes *you* happy. Including: live.

affirming beauty and not enough on deconstructing its necessity." She goes on to share an experience she had on Facebook: A friend published a post that said, "I'm not pretty and I'm fine with that." What of course followed was a barrage of comments from "misguided" though well-meaning friends who insisted she was being "ridiculous" and *of course* she was pretty. Lindsay describes her discomfort with and defensiveness about this type of forceful response: "Here was a woman moving away from an oppressive and harmful hierarchy, and with the best of intentions, her friends were trying to drag her back in."[1]

Now, let me explain how I break this down in my world. The words "beautiful" and "pretty" mean two different things to me. Beauty is something that is everywhere. The sunset is beautiful. Human connection is beautiful. Kindness is beautiful. Bodies are beautiful—all of them. Beauty is ubiquitous, inherent, and found in all of us: on the outside and the inside.

The word "pretty," however, when used to describe a woman's physical appearance, signifies to me a physical ideal that's fabricated by companies to make you believe that you'll never be enough until you reach it. Pretty is what they want you to believe in. Pretty is what causes women to battle each other. Pretty has been created to always be exclusive. Pretty is a made-up lie created to line the pockets of money-hungry assholes. SO. FUCK. PRETTY.

Reclaim beauty.

Now, there's nothing wrong with wanting to feel attractive, and part of learning to love your body usually includes learning how to feel good about your appearance, defining your romantic and sexual identity, redefining what attractive means to you, and yes, maybe even feeling "pretty." Many women find the body positive world while chasing their need to feel "pretty" and there is *nothing* wrong with this! I'm cool with whatever it takes to bring us all into this magical realm of body lovin'! But at the end of the day, body acceptance and positivity are about so much more. I think Lindsay has a point in that allowing our quest for feeling attractive to be our *only* defining factor or goal doesn't get us far enough towards our end destination.

You feel?

So regardless of why you may have started (or want to start) your body love journey and what you'd like to get out of it, it's important to also see the bigger picture: Body love is critical to the health (mental, emotional, and physical) of our whole world on a big scale. Learning to love your body is ridiculously complex, and it affects more than just ourselves and those immediately nearby. It affects the entire globe and all of its venerable systemic issues; a world that starts to invest in body love has the capability to shift to a more equal, compassionate, and kind place.

Sonya Renee Taylor, founder of The Body Is Not An Apology, addresses this notion in the comment section under "Pretty Unnecessary":

[The Body Is Not An Apology is] not invested in whether people find themselves "pretty" or "attractive." [It is] is an international movement committed to cultivating global Radical Self Love and Body Empowerment. We believe that discrimination, social inequality, and injustice are manifestations of our inability to make peace with the body, our own and others. Through information dissemination, personal and social transformation projects and community building, The Body Is Not An Apology fosters global, radical, unapologetic self-love which translates to radical human love and action in service toward a more just, equitable and compassionate world. We are most concerned with how our relationship with ourselves serves as the foundation for interrupting body based oppression. We indeed believe in the inherent "beauty" of all humans but as Lindsay shared, not from a lens that is about aesthetics but about inherent value and worth.[2]

To which I say: YES.

HOLY YES, SONYA.

Sonya perfectly encapsulates why body love is so important: When we foster appreciation for and love ourselves, we start to contribute to the world in a way that allows equality, inclusivity, and all forms of kindness.

Part of my job includes speaking to all kinds of college groups, and I often circle back to this exact concept: Loving your body can change the world. Not just your world (which is super important *and* reason enough), but the *entire* world.

It sounds farfetched, I know, but I'm sayin' this with a straight face.

In my lecture, "Change the World, Love Your Body: The Social Impact of Body Love," I always begin by asking how many people in the room would feel comfortable looking me in the eye and calling themselves beautiful. Beautiful/handsome/attractive, whatever the word of choice is for them. Consistently, a small percentage shyly raise their hands. I'm always thrilled to see the hands, but never surprised by those who *don't* feel confident enough to join in. This group is most certainly not alone in their insecurities. Globally, the statistic of women that would call themselves beautiful is 4 percent.[3] **Four.**

Holy shit, y'all. You following this?

Now, the study uses the word "beautiful" to mean "pretty," and, as we know, "pretty" is a social construct. But we're going to meet the world where it's at and go with the terminology they use. The purpose behind this question is to ask who feels physically valid. Confident in their bodies. "Enough." With that in mind, 4 percent makes me incredibly sad.

But wait. There's more! We also see devastating statistics around this issue and the fear we have about being the opposite of "pretty," which is most often associated with thin.

Here's the state of our world's body image issues in five bullet points:

- 81 percent of ten-year-olds are afraid of being fat.
- These ten-year-olds are more afraid of becoming fat than they are of cancer, war, or losing both of their parents.[4]
- In a survey of girls nine and ten years old, 40 percent have tried to lose weight.[5]
- 91 percent of women are unhappy with their bodies and resort to dieting.[6]
- And 5 percent of women naturally possess the body type often portrayed by Americans in the media.[7]

So essentially, we have the majority of our fourth and fifth graders terrified of a body type that we've told them is wrong, and they're more afraid of becoming this shape than of most anything else. They're also dieting to avoid a vilified body before their body has even had a chance to develop. That doesn't go away, as the *vast* majority of grown-ass women don't like their bodies and actively try to change them by dieting. But most of this emotional pain and distress is for naught, because only 5 percent of women have a body type that could ever give them the *chance* to look like the model we're all striving to emulate. Which (by the power of very simple math) means we can safely assume that 95 percent of women's bodies will naturally refuse to become that which we see portrayed by the media as desirable, no matter what they do. Which leaves almost all ladies stuck in a cycle of trying and failing and trying and failing to become something they physically *can't.*

Now if that above paragraph isn't fucked up, I don't know what is. And I just might have more fucked-up-ness for you. What do we see happen to people's lives because of those five statistics I shared above?

We develop low self-esteem. People have really terrible, horrible, no good, very bad days . . . just because of their perception of their bodies.

As a result, we suffer employment losses. Those who have low self-esteem make considerably less money than their confident counterparts. They also take fewer risks, and I would imagine with that magnitude of insecurity they are far less successful in reaching their goals.

We put our lives on hold. How many of us have waited to do something until we've lost weight? *I'll buy jeans AFTER I lose ten pounds. I'll do family photos AFTER I . . . I'll start dating AFTER I . . .* We painfully stunt our lives because we have decided that our bodies are simply not good enough to work with now. The progress that's lost because of this? Tragic.

We establish poor relationship skills. When we dislike our bodies, we tend to feel unlovable and undeserving. Feeling this way can affect our relationships in a lot of ways, from not approaching those we're interested in to staying in abusive relationships much longer than we should.

We can create or trigger mental illness. Extremely low self-esteem and self-hatred can often trigger larger mental issues, and perhaps even cause a mental disorder to develop that is significant enough to smother happiness and growth. Although many mental disorders (including but not limited to bipolar disorder, schizophrenia, anxiety, and yes, depression) are the result of biological imbalances, we're capable of escalating such imbalances and impeding our emotional and mental growth. Eating disorders included.

We commit suicide. And sadly, there is case after case of this: people who would rather die than live in the body the world has told them is inferior.

All this is certainly cataclysmic, but let's take a moment to think about the flip side of each of these issues . . . if people LOVED their bodies, they might have *higher self-esteem.* They could grab life by the horns and *go after their goals right now.* They could feel lovable and have healthy intimate relationships. They might feel more confident at work and take more career leaps. They might be able to temper or even eliminate a self-triggered mental disorder (even though disorders won't ever go away entirely, those triggered by self-loathing would surely be fewer!), and ideally, they would celebrate life instead of ending it, because they would truly believe they are good enough just the way they are now.

Now, that's all great, but imagine if not only one person, but *everyone* started doing these things. Living, loving, taking risks, investing in themselves and others . . . billions of people doing this together would most certainly shift the face of the world we live in. This is what Sonya Renee Taylor was talking about in her comment. Body love really can contribute to the elimination of hate, competition, inequality, oppression, invisibility . . . creating opportunity and space for all.

Believe it.

So, my goal in life as an advocate is not to necessarily make you feel "pretty" (though if you need permission to go ahead and feel pretty, it's yours!) but rather to inform, educate, and empower so you can make decisions about your body that are comfortable and right for you specifically. THIS IS WHAT BODY LOVE IS. When people feel in complete control of their bodies, minds, and worth, body love has truly come to stay. When we find total body autonomy for every individual, those magical things mentioned above really can happen. And that magic will ripple out until it affects everyone in a positive sense. It's that big of a deal. I'll say it again: Body love has the capacity to change the world.

Hopefully this book can be a game changer for you, but it is by no means the be-all and end-all of body image exploration; far from it. It's not even the ultimate book of empowering things for fat chicks. The body activism world is multifaceted, and there is a lot of information out there that I suggest you find and ponder. This particular book is a collection of *my* realizations, epiphanies, and *aha!* moments interspersed with facts and thoughts that I wish I'd known and had earlier. I want to share these things with you because after embracing body love I have found considerably more fulfillment, purpose, love, and sense of worthiness.

Listen up, because this is important: You deserve to have these things, too. Your size is irrelevant to your ability to find fulfillment, purpose, love, a sense of worthiness, and the ovaries to not give a fuck.

I deserve it and you deserve it . . . so read on, my friend. Read on.

✳

start now, GODDAMNIT: waiting doesn't work

[CHAPTER TWO]

Sorry I yelled.

It's just REALLY that important.

One of the traps we fall into as humans (flawed creatures that we are) is the one I mentioned in the last chapter, the one where we decide we're going to (fill in the blank with important life activity) *AFTER* we lose *x* number of pounds. Or maybe instead of losing pounds, it's building muscle. Or burning fat. *Whatever it is,* the issue is that we limit our lives because we refuse to do something good, great, or needed *until* we change our bodies.

There are a lot of fucked-up things about this situation, y'all.

I did a phone interview for a confidence website written by teens, and after a chat about the basics of body love, the young interviewer shared her personal story with me. One of the things that resonated with me *real hard* (and will for many others, I'm sure) was when she said, "I kept telling myself I would do this and that after I lose weight, and I just got so *tired . . . so tired* of making myself promises that I knew I could never keep."

OMG I KNOW THAT EXHAUSTION. The skyrocketing hope that lasts for sixty seconds because *this time* you're gonna become a better version of you and THEN *everything will be okay*. And then comes the exhaustion after trying so hard yet still feeling inadequate, which only reminds you how much you truly hate yourself.

It's a really sad thing.

The saddest part is we do this to ourselves over and over again. Things I hear often: I'll take those family photos once I lose 10 pounds: I'll look better then. I'll start dating again once I lose 10 pounds:

> **Real talk: Your life is not going to become more amazing, happier, or more successful after you lose those 10 pounds. Or 20 pounds. Or 50 pounds.**

More people will reply to my profile. I'll join the gym, but only after I lose 10 pounds on my own first: I don't want to be embarrassed. I'll buy this dress, but only after I lose 10 pounds: I can't bring myself to buy something *that* big.

Real talk: Your life is not going to become happier, more amazing, or more successful after you lose those 10 pounds. Or 20 pounds. Or 50 pounds. Because the pounds aren't *really* the issue. Your state of mind is.

Here. Allow me to illustrate with a super-duper personal story. Because that's what I do best.

While searching for some old college essays a little bit ago, I stumbled upon a forgotten online photo album that held forty-eight pages of memories from my last ten years. I was thrilled to find this photographic treasure chest and eagerly clicked through, reliving every moment I had captured. It's so strange, the things old photos can evoke. I could somehow remember the smell of my dorm room, the dust in the abandoned apartments upstairs, that particular monsoon season, those nights smoking cloves in a hoodie, that visit to a park in Baltimore, those tears shed on top of a parking garage, that drive to nowhere, those feelings of hopelessness, that moment of ecstatic joy, that trip to the museum for the Renoir exhibit, that afternoon spent listening to Jenny Watson and drinking High Life in the backyard, that week spent on the circus train, and that cup of espresso in Venice. The evolution of me becoming who I am today was laid out in front of me: my many faces and multiple facets. It all came back to me with such force, it nearly knocked the breath out of me. It was unexpectedly powerful.

Then I noticed how beautiful I was in all these old pictures—and I immediately connected this with how much thinner I used to be. I wasn't skinny, but I wasn't fat, and this shocked my nervous system in a way I can't explain. I became hyperaware of how uncomfortable I felt sitting in my current body, and how I didn't see that body reflected in any of the photos on my screen. I was instantly attacked by those cruel teachings of society that I've internalized my entire life. I wasn't necessarily fat back then—maybe just bigger than some. So why did I remember always feeling like I was twice the size that I was? How was my body dysmorphia (exaggerated or imagined perception of one's physical flaws) so extreme that I felt like I was an embarrassment to those around me? Why did I hate myself so much when I looked that great? How could I not see how *beautiful I was back then*? Maybe I'm even more of a failure now than I was then, and maybe I should lose weight to become like Old Me again. Maybe I would meet more people if I looked like Old Me. Maybe I would succeed more if I looked like Old Me. Maybe I would be happier if I looked like Old Me. Maybe Old Me was better.

And then I caught myself.

I realized that Old Me hated everything about herself. I can see the beauty so clearly now, but she had no idea. She loathed every part of her body and wished she could trade it in for anything else. Anything. Her self-esteem was nonexistent, though she pretended this wasn't the case. Old Me wanted to die instead of live in that body, and I wish I could have hugged her and told her how exquisite she was.

And then I started to sob.

I sobbed for the girl who was so beautiful on both the inside and the outside but couldn't see it. I sobbed for the girl who spent years missing out on magical parts of life because her perspective was poisoned. I sobbed for the girl who repeatedly punished herself for not being good enough. And I sobbed for every other girl out there who believes the same lies that she did. I sobbed because these lies destroy lives.

And then my answer came. Retrieving the body of Old Me wouldn't change a thing. I'm fatter than I have ever been yet somehow happier than I have ever been. I have a career and a mission in life. I have more fulfilling relationships. I am solid in my beliefs. I have more positive attention. I have people who love me, a lover who wants me, and goals that I'm achieving.

I am the happiest I have ever been, and this simply proves that **happiness is not a size**. Happiness is a state of being. Happiness is about finding what you love about yourself and sharing it. Happiness is about taking what you hate about yourself and learning to love it. Happiness is an internal sanctuary where you are enough just as you are, right now.

A webcomic site called Toothpaste for Dinner has one comic that shows a fat man who says, "I hate myself." The next frame shows him as a skinny man saying, "Nope, that wasn't it."[1] Every time I read it I smile at that profound truth. All too often we decide that we'll love ourselves "just the way we are" . . . but only after we change. The reality is our dissatisfaction with our bodies isn't a physical issue; it's a mental barrier, and until we address that root problem we will find ourselves looking in the mirror with a frown on our face no matter our size. Complete and total body acceptance is the key to changing our perspective on life, and it starts on the inside.

We can't treat our minds and bodies well until we learn to love them. Nothing good comes out of finding the flaws and harboring resentment towards ourselves. I was conventionally stunning and hated everything about my body, hurting it repeatedly on purpose. I am unconventionally beautiful now, and I find myself with more good days than bad. I'm loving myself. Just the way I am. Right now. And I am happy.

And isn't that what it's all about?

Well, it is for me.

Transformative moment number 587 (out of a kajillion) on my body love journey happened the day I stopped looking for a model in the mirror. I never realized that up until that point, I was expecting to see "pretty" in my reflection. This delusional expectation only served to reinforce everything that I thought I wasn't. Instead of unique beauty, what I focused on was my double chin, thunder thighs, pronounced belly, imperfect arms . . . all of them shockingly disappointing as I looked for a thinner, photoshopped version of myself. And guess what? I never saw her.

I wish I could tell you the magic moment when my thinking changed, but all I know is eventually I allowed myself to see my body for what it truly was . . . and that was when I started to develop an appreciation for what I have. I now look for *myself* in the mirror, and I'm never disappointed. I see my body in all its atypical glory, and most days it just feels oh so right! Nothing was altered except my expectation; to everyone else I looked exactly the same. But to me, that shift changed everything. Internal power, y'all. We gotz it.

I'm painfully aware of the fact that I have apologized for my body for over two decades. Verbally—excusing myself for taking up so much space. Making jokes about what I was eating. Turning down compliments because I didn't feel deserving. And physically—wearing black, long-sleeved shirts in the Arizona summer. Shying away from anything loud, flashy, or sparkly. Basically doing anything I could to minimize the presence of my body. What a way to live, huh? And sadly, I think we can all relate on some level. I look back on those years of my life now and shake my head. It's as if I thought I was keeping the fact that I was fat a secret by attempting to disguise it. As if those who saw me in black would then see me in bright colors and gasp, "HOLY SHIT! UNTIL NOW, I HAD NO IDEA SHE WAS FAT!" Illogical. Our bodies cannot truly be hidden, no matter how many black outfits we wear. No matter how many pairs of Spanx we

THE
**FAT
PEOPLE:**
do all the things!
CHALLENGE

✳

#1 CANNONBALL

If anything, you would think fat people would be THE BEST at cannonballing. It's pure science, isn't it? More surface area = bigger splash. I can only assume fat people are not supposed to cannonball for fear of flooding the entire town they live in, but I don't believe it. So, I very selfishly put the safety of a million people at risk while I tested this theory. And guess what? Fat people can safely cannonball! No need to pull out the emergency kits and rafts just yet. I jumped ten more times just for the hell of it. Still no flood, just more fun. Though I do need to work on my cannonball face . . . it's far too serious.

Your challenge: Do a cannonball yourself! Suit up (or do it nude for extra points), and just *try* and flood your town. I dare you.

own. No matter how much we suck it in. Doesn't it seem like a better use of our time to just accept the fact that our bodies are our bodies and live our lives like there is no tomorrow? I'm pretty sure the answer is yes.

Now, because honesty is important to me, I try to share all of my raw and real moments on my blog. Obviously, I don't have a video camera with a constant live feed, so there are always parts of my life that are not written about or covered (I also appreciate an element of privacy, albeit a small one). But I share both the fun and the hard stuff. I attempt to write candidly and with vulnerability, because, y'know what? We all need a little bit more of that in our lives. We live in a made-over world that's groomed and preened, and so often we look outside and say . . . man, I wish I had my shit together, too. But the reality is nobody has all their shit together, not in every area of their life—not in *most* areas of their lives. So when you share the shit you *don't* have together? People relate. They connect. And all of a sudden, they don't feel so alone.

Social scientist Brené Brown often lectures and writes about vulnerability and our critical need for it if we are to make any kind of progress. In her book *The Gifts of Imperfection: Let Go of Who You Think You're Supposed to Be and Embrace Who You Are,* she says, "Owning our story can be hard but not nearly as difficult as spending our lives running from it."[2] Opening ourselves up and being willing to look at the hard stuff in life makes space for change, and learning how to *welcome* vulnerability? That's where everything good starts.

So work with me on this.

I'm here to share with you what I have learned, and hopefully you'll find ways to apply it in your life. It may not be easy to read and take to heart (though it's not all hard either), but all of it's important. So, if you're committed to taking this body love journey with me through the next two hundred pages, I'm gonna suggest that you open yourself up to being vulnerable. Vulnerable in the sense that you are going to set down your defense weapons and lower your walls. That you're going to forget what you've been told just for a moment and be open to new ideas. That you're going to look deep inside even when it's scary and acknowledge that *maybe* you don't have all your shit together. That you're going to use your critical mind and explore how this may apply to you. Vulnerable in the sense that you are open to the idea that no one is perfect, you're not alone, and maybe, just maybe, if you open your heart a little bit you can start to love yourself. The hardest things in life are mended with vulnerability.

And of course, it's best to make that commitment to be vulnerable and start the journey to loving yourself . . .

NOW.

LIVING THE DREAM AT 250 POUNDS OR "WHY DIET CULTURE IS FULL OF SHIT AND CAN SUCK MY LADY DICK"

VIRGIE TOVAR OF #LOSEHATENOTWEIGHT

I have a *major* fucking problem with diet culture. I can give you my technical, academic definition of "diet culture," but let's skip that for now. Diet culture is the voice in your head that tells you not to eat that cookie with an urgency that feels life-threatening. It's the reason you shared that piece of cheesecake with not one, but four of your closest friends—and why you guys *still* left the last bite. It's why grown women lie on the fitting room floor with bloodied finger tips attempting to zip up a pair of jeans. Diet culture is the reason weight loss is at the top of everyone's New Year's resolutions lists. Everyone hates dieting, but we still feel this thrill when we eat a carrot or get our dressing on the side. And even though we pay our bills, own cars, hold jobs, have children, and manage relationships, every day we allow diet culture to treat us like we're five-year-olds who can't make decisions about when or how much to eat.

That thrill is no accident. That shame is no accident. We've learned to feel these things through a sophisticated system of rewards and punishments. Some call it oppression. Some call it conditioning. Some might even call it Stockholm Syndrome. Let's just call it bullshit for short. And that's really where my problem resides: that bullshit begets bullshit. That's what diet culture is and always will be. Diet culture is bigger than any one individual diet or dieter; it pervades almost every facet of our lives. I urge you to try and imagine going one single, solitary day without hearing someone talk about weight loss or calories or fucking *gluten*. Can you do it? I can't. And I live in a feminist bubble in the middle of San Francisco! That's how you know something is a culture—when it's unavoidable and you've stopped knowing or even caring about why there are rules, but you follow them anyway.

I used to follow these rules, chasing every diet trend, calorically restricting to the point of making myself ill, and feeling that blissed-out joy when I lost a pound. For a long, long time I wanted to lose weight more than I wanted *anything* else, and I believed life would begin later. I would wear a bikini later. I would be happy later. I would fall in love, wear cute clothes, feel beautiful, wear red lipstick, travel, enjoy cake, smile in pictures—later. Then one day I had a major break-through. I was sitting at my kitchen table, feeling really good about myself because I just done this intense workout. I was panting and sweating profusely, and I was dreaming about the day when I would be thin enough to eat dessert. So I asked myself: *How much longer until I can eat some damn cake?*

A year? No.

Five years? No.

Ten years? No.

I kept going like that in my head until I reached the end of my life, and I realized that was the answer. The dieting might never end, because if I stopped I could gain weight, and in my mind that would have meant I had lost. That would have meant my life was worth-less. I truly believed that being thin was the most important thing I could ever achieve. I believed that once I became thin my world would change, that everything would make sense, and that I would literally be perfect. This is called "magical thinking," and the suspension of disbe-lief is the engine upon which diet culture runs.

Dieting was many things to me: It was often difficult and soul draining, but it also made me feel good and, somehow, safe. I real-ize now dieting was my way of communicating to myself and others that I wanted to be "normal." Dieting was my way of communicating my understanding that my fat body was unacceptable and shameful. It was my way of communicating that I understood a woman's role is to be small and totally obsessed with how little space and resources she could take up. Dieting represented a way I could create meaning in my life, but the problem is you can't create meaning by obsessing about kale or calories or what the tag on your pants says.

Dieting is about forever placing our eyes on a future where our goal is to be someone we are not, and never living now. Dieting is about obedience and submission—to a rule that says you are worth nothing more than the number on your scale. Dieting limits our lives. In the rules of dieting lives the centuries-old legacy of the second-class citizenship of women. These are the same rules that have kept women from achieving amazing things for too long. The truth is that a woman who is singularly obsessed with how she looks **will never be an independent woman.**

We deserve more than that. You deserve more than that.

And that was the biggest realization I've ever had: that my body is mine, this life is mine, and no bullshit set of rules is going to take that from me. I no longer sweat at my kitchen table dreaming of cake and joy and love. Now I am a wearer of short skirts and red lipstick, an activist dedicated to eradicating diet culture, a lover of fine French and Italian pastries, a world traveler, the proud owner of seven two-piece bathing suits, a San Francisco bohemian who adores pedicures, cheetah print, and Chihuahuas, and couldn't live without huge accessories and huger sunglasses. At 250 pounds, I'm actually living the life I was convinced only dieting could give me. The thing is: Diets were *never* going to give me that life.

Only I could.

✳

you hate your body because don draper told you to: throw some shade at history

[CHAPTER THREE]

Don't get too pissed at Don, though. It was really his predecessors who came up with the bullshit marketing plans that trained people to hate themselves, live restricted lives based on an impossible-to-attain ideal, and even, in some cases, kill themselves (literally) trying to reach it, or because they couldn't reach it. Don didn't come up with these ideals of beauty—he just perpetuated them.

Okay, actually, get pissed. Maybe even really pissed.

We're all aware that when it comes to physical appearance, our society is a fucking bully. But I always wanted to know *why*. Why is our structure this way? Why are fat people bullied, often to the point of suicide? And why are women singled out for body shame? Why have we all learned to hate ourselves? *How THE FUCK did we get here*?

After my own realization that even in this world I could learn to love myself as I am, I immersed myself in reading that supported this theory. Self-help books, women's issues books, feminist theory books, health books, and history books. Guess which kind of book was the catalyst for one of the most pivotal turning points in my journey? History books. *Motherfucking history books.* They changed everything.

I thrive on facts: They speak to me, I trust in them. Sure, the cheerful body love memes online can help a little on the self-love journey, but they aren't enough—for me, they're not a game changer, and are easily forgotten. I want something solid to prove why something is, so I can use that information to better my life. Only then do things start to shift for me. Oh, you too? GOOD, because I'm about to school you in a way you've never been schooled before.

Buckle up, bitches. I'm about to blow your mind.

This "why" comes from several moments in history, and to be honest . . . they're all a little complicated. There's nothing simple about civilization's sordid, oppressive, and money-driven past. It's also a very long story, so I'm just going to share the CliffsNotes version of several very large chunks of history, each of which we could probably talk about for days. The *reason* I'm sharing this with you is to give some insight into three significant questions about body image: (1) Why are women the ones we often talk about when it comes to body image? (2) Where does our "thin is always better" mentality came from and (3) Where did the perpetuation of the ideal body we see today start?

The first question can be answered by exploring the history of farming communities.

Part 1: Farming and the Development of Patriarchy

Historians believe that early human civilization was made up of nomadic hunter-gatherers and structured as an egalitarian society, with no chiefs or leaders. Women had their super specific roles: They took care of the children, nurtured the community, and kept everyone connected. And men's priorities focused on awesome stuff like hunting and fertilization. Y'know. The fun chores.

It's said that because early humans had to move constantly for survival, it didn't make sense to have a food "stash" that would need to be guarded; the food they had on hand was only what they could carry. And because of all the travel, women were careful to have children only about every four years to ensure the youngest child was able to walk on their own with the group before another came along. This, as you can imagine, significantly limited family size.

The transition from hunter-gatherers to farmers was long and tenuous, according to many. No one woke up one day and said, "HEY, WE SHOULD DO THIS THING AND CALL IT FARMING!" It was fucking slow and messy progress. Farming wasn't discovered or invented; it evolved based on needs. Gradually, as farming was adopted more and more, the accumulation of food was possible, and with the accumulation of food came denser populations.

To put it simply: As humans had the opportunity to store food, they also had the opportunity to survive severe winters and other life-threatening situations. They could farm during the plentiful seasons and survive the harsh ones using the food they could now amass. And amass they did! As soon as food could be reserved and kept for future survival, the need to have *more* food for *longer* survival became paramount. And an acknowledgment of class distinction began: Those who had more would live longer, and were therefore more powerful. Those who had less were less powerful and had a lower chance of survival. This, in essence, is where class systems may have first come into play.

Because of the desire to climb to the top and the need to access resources to do so, some historians say that crops became of utmost importance, and *more* farmers were needed to generate more product. With this quest, then, women became the "farmer-making machines," and therefore coveted property. Unlike during the hunter-gatherer period, women could now have as many children as they could feed, which allowed for large families of future farmers to develop.

As female bodies turned into property, virginity became a desirable trait (it was essentially a promise that the woman hadn't "given" any farmers to someone else), and it's often said that this is how patriarchal rule was interwoven into the growing society. Women (property) were now at a distinct disadvantage, which is part of the reason we see the gender injustice that we do today. Because women were minimized then, they continue to be so today.[1] That loss of power and influence is why, in part, marketing and advertising specifically targets women and their role in society. Now, know that this is historical conjecture, as hunter-gatherers and farmers didn't exactly hand over their diaries to us, but this theory is supported by many scholars and certainly warrants a few moments (or more) of consideration.

Part 2: The Slenderization for Class Distinction

In the early to mid-1800s the United States was in quite the predicament: Food was scarce, so people with larger bodies tended to be wealthier and had enough to eat. Because of that, they were thought to be healthier.

In her essay, "The Inner Corset: A Brief History of Fat in the United States," Laura Fraser lets us in on the secret:

> *Once upon a time, a man with a thick gold watch swaying*
> *from a big, round paunch was the very picture of American*
> *prosperity and vigor. Accordingly . . . years ago, a beautiful*
> *woman had plump cheeks and arms, and she wore a . . . bustle*
> *to emphasize her full, substantial hips. Women were sexy if*
> *they were heavy. In those days, Americans knew that a layer*
> *of fat was a sign that you could afford to eat well and that you*
> *stood a better chance of fighting off infectious diseases than*
> *most people.*

But that all changed very quickly.

In the late 1800s, advances in transportation made it easier to distribute food widely. With this came an influx of large groups of immigrant workers, many of whom had shorter, stockier bodies. The visibility of stockier bodies, combined with the food influx, meant that now most Americans were able to "fill out," and the gap between the large wealthy bodies and the smaller poor bodies began to close. The *upper class* soon sought a way to differentiate themselves and reclaim their social power over the lower classes, and they did this partially by idealizing thinness. Adding to this, people romanticized the frail bodies of several European artists at the time who had tuberculosis, and soon Americans were grabbing onto the NEW ideal: slenderness as a form of class distinction.

No longer was it best to be fat: Thin bodies became all the rage, a sign of prosperity and style.

Previously, the medical field had warned of a link between thinness and certain disorders, and cautioned women against losing too much weight. Now, society's tune had changed: The fashionable figure was suddenly a slender one that seemed liberated and elite, and, even though at first doctors didn't endorse this obsession with thinness (in fact, they fought it), eventually they caved to societal pressure and the chance to make money by remedying patients. But disgust with fat bodies was created by the people, not doctors. People, and, well, the U.S. economy.

One former president of the American Academy of Medicine named Woods Hutchinson bemoaned this flighty shift in support of the skinny ideal. In a 1926 edition of the *Saturday Evening Post* he said, "Fashion has apparently the backing of grave physicians, of food reformers and physical trainers, and even of great insurance companies, all chanting in unison the new commandment of fashion: 'Thou shalt be thin!'"[3]

There are still countries where the fat woman or an "atypical" body is the traditional ideal, but we, the United States of America, are most certainly not one of them. We are a country that obsesses about dieting and weight in a phenomenal way, and it's directly because of our history.

Laura Fraser clarifies: "Thinness is, at its heart, a peculiarly American preoccupation. Europeans admire slenderness, but without our Puritanism they have more relaxed and moderate attitudes about food, eating, and body size (the British are most like us in both being heavy and fixating on weight loss schemes)."

Reading homework? *The Fat Studies Reader*, edited by Esther Rothblum and Sondra Solovay.[4]

Part 3: Perfection as an Economic Life Raft

We now live in a world where it is acceptable for women to vote, own land, make decisions about reproductive health, start a company, choose a single lifestyle, have copious amounts of sex, and run for prolific positions in government. But there is still one thing that is heavily contested by most communities, government, the medical field, and the media: women who have a body that lies outside our mandated thin, young, white, able bodied, and, consequently, "pretty" standard.

Beauty ideals have existed as long as patriarchy, and every generation has had to fight its own version (cold creams and cosmetics to imitate film stars popped up long before World War II and were sold to young ladies with money to spend), but there was a point in history when the standard of beauty became an insidious political weapon used to hinder the advancement of women no matter their age or status. This particular segment is directly related to World War II.

As men were drafted, their absence created a large labor need, and the country encouraged (middle-class, white) women to fill it. These women took over jobs in factories and there learned that they were capable of much more than they ever knew. When the men returned, three million women then left the workforce and returned to the home with a new shift in consciousness.

In order to divert the female attention away from their previous work success, the concept of the "feminine mystique" was sold to every soon-to-be "June Cleaver" in America. The feminine mystique was the idea that a woman had just three roles in life: to be a good wife, a good mother, and a good homemaker. This relegated women to one area of life, keeping them preoccupied and entrenched in their newfound purpose. Magazines were influential and targeted women, capitalizing on "guilt over hidden dirt," and yes, various cosmetics to assist in becoming the "hot wife" their husband "deserved." Marketers made out like bandits by selling products to every female desperate to become the perfect domestic goddess. (A note: this "feminine mystique" or focus on women in the home was prominently sold to white females, as women from non-white backgrounds and ethnicities had almost all been working-class up until that point.)

Not surprisingly, many women who subscribed to the domestic trend eventually found themselves miserable while trying to exist within these limited identity confines, and the lure of employment started to glisten in the distance. When these women started to leave vacuuming, cooking dinner, and helping with homework for office work, advertisers needed to find a new gimmick, a new, evergreen, "briefcase-sized neurosis"—as Naomi Wolf puts it in *The Beauty Myth: How Images of Beauty Are Used Against Women*—that women could take with them to work.[6]

And thus, two new brilliant industries were emphasized like never before: **Beauty and Youth.**

The beauty and youth "religion" replaced the religion of domesticity, and, while the products changed, the invasion tactic was the same: Instead of being a heroine by raising children, you could now reach the same idol status by becoming beautiful (or, as we've established, "pretty"). Advertising agencies created a perfect version of a women that didn't exist, doesn't exist, and will never exist, and preached the gospel that in order to be okay, you must reach that (unattainable) ideal.

AND WOMEN BOUGHT IT. And we continue to buy it today.

After all, our bodies will *always* be with us, and we will *always* grow older. I mean, it's sickeningly brilliant and it's making billions upon billions of dollars as we speak. So, with that, I high-five the men on Madison Avenue for inventing a genius, exclusionary, and lucrative scheme, while simultaneously punching them in the crotch as hard as I can for ruining so many lives in the pursuit of money. Because of them, most of us are still imprisoned in our bodies.

The most frightening part of all? As females (and people in general) gradually find new ways to fight oppression and gain freedom from old rules, the myth of the "beauty ideal" keeps evolving to keep them distracted and entrenched in self-loathing. It's important to note that, while the focal points of the beauty ideal often change to maintain maximum control, several prerequisites have always been mandatory since the politicization of this ploy: thinness, whiteness, youthfulness, and the "flawlessness" that comes from visual alteration of photographs. ALL of these are still relevant today. Right here. Right now. But in *addition* to this, we also see a "social reflex," or a new way to suppress women and their self-esteem whenever liberation is found. This has been a historical constant.

For example: when women decided to liberate themselves from the overly feminine look, magazines endorsed the "nude look" so women could look "natural" while still subscribing to the standard of pretty that they were trying to avoid. When women started to reclaim their reproductive rights, it is no coincidence that the average model weight dropped to 23 percent below the average woman's weight. But, as we silly women are wont to do, we've continued to liberate ourselves in new ways, year after year. And, so. In response, there's an always-evolving "beauty myth" (or definition of "pretty" and "desirable") that introduces a new domination technique to compensate for each of our newfound powers.

What about today? Well, my generation (and the ones immediately surrounding it, to a certain extent) has become somewhat obsessed with visual diversity and inclusion. Because of this we are starting to see more "alternative" bodies in the mainstream. Most notably, we're now seeing plus-size women in some fashion spreads. Because we're seeing some larger bodies in magazines and online, the standard of beauty is definitely shifting, but our new alteration of the beauty ideal is so insidious that most of us don't even realize that it's still keeping us preoccupied, insecure, and in a constant state of self-hatred. It's exactly as Naomi Wolf said: The beauty myth uses appearance to direct behavior. It's not about a woman's appearance at all, but rather the tractability of the person who tries to attain perfection.[7]

Our current obsession is with a figure that *BuzzFeed* calls the "postmodern beauty." What does our perfect body look like today? It's a combination of thin, but not *scary* super-thin; athletic, but only the kind that looks like you do yoga; strong but not too muscular; feminine; having a "thigh gap," but not the "heroin chic" kind from the '90s; curvy, but still perfectly proportional; sexy, with boobs, but dear god not like Pamela Anderson (have some class already); poreless, but naturally so; and with a fit body that we see everywhere. Our society places the most value on a body that, without speaking, screams: HEALTH, VIBRANT HEALTH AND WELLNESS IS WHAT I EMBODY.

I'm here to propose something that I believe too few of us realize: **"Health" is our new "beauty myth."**

Health, and, by extension, fitness and wellness. *So says the super fat chick who loves cronuts,* many will scoff. This is most certainly not a popular opinion. Culturally, we tend to believe all diagnoses, opinions, and commentary from all medical "professionals." We don't fuck with or question *anything* about health and medicine, including our infatuation with it. This, dear friends, at *the very least*, deserves questioning. And the reading of Chapter 5.

In the last few decades we, societally, have created some space to unpack the issues around body image. We've now had the conversation about how extreme eating disorders like anorexia nervosa aren't healthy so many times that some countries have started banning "unnaturally thin" bodies of a "skeleton" nature from runways, movies,

#2: SWING.

I did this challenge, and I REALLY enjoyed it. It was a beautiful Tucson day, and I walked to a nearby park for some swinging. It is fucking awesome to see how high you can get. Did the swing set break? Not even slightly.

Your challenge: Find a swing set near you! Anyone (there are no size exclusions) can join in. Bring a pillow for comfort if needed, because let's be real: That plastic isn't cozy.

and fashion spreads. We claim to be offended when this type of body surfaces and have no hesitation judging those bodies against the same ruler we use for fat bodies. Today, everyone seem to say: "Fat is horrifying, but *so is the extreme opposite*. It's important for EVERYONE TO BE HEALTHY!" This, my friends, is a perfect example of how health has become one of our main obsessions.

Now, preoccupation with exercise and healthy living isn't anything new. Not even remotely. Remember the '80s with aerobics, toned supermodel arms, and the wearing of sneakers with a dress suit? We've always valued health and wellness to an extent. After all, we've always had bodies that need maintenance, and we on a fundamental level want to take care of them! So, then, what's the difference? The *difference* between then and now is that our obsession with worth in relation to health is at an all-time high. Never before have we judged people's value, morality, and meaningfulness by their medical charts and their ability to run marathons.

This can be starkly highlighted by an Instagram account with over sixty thousand followers whose name and message is literally, "Healthy is the new skinny." This is EXACTLY the issue. Plus-size workout companies also push this concept. Hard. We have replaced

Fen-Phen, Slimfast, and melba toast with the Paleo diet, CrossFit, and juicing. Now, don't misunderstand. There isn't anything inherently wrong with "clean eating," strengthening exercises, or juicing. No way. It is our worshipping and utilization of them in order to become the ideal and "worthy" body type (and the guilt that comes if we don't) that is the issue.

It's fascinating how we've been fooled into feeling like we're reclaiming power by saying DON'T WORRY ABOUT YOUR SIZE, ONLY YOUR HEALTH! But really, what we're doing is taking the exact same process of body oppression and giving it a new name.

Our "diet industry" has become a "lifestyle change industry." Same concept. Same strategy. Same outcome. Different mask.

It's rather effective. Think about how easily and automatically this excludes various groups of people. Who is instantly exiled the second health becomes the top measurement of worth? People with physical disabilities. People with chronic or incurable ailments. People who live in poverty and can't afford balanced meals. People who don't have the resources or education required to learn about how to take care of their bodies. People who live with a mental illness that doesn't allow them to take care of themselves at all. People so focused on just surviving that there isn't any energy left to focus on physical maintenance. Lots and lots of people who are unable to fully participate in our "wellness culture" because of the body and life they were born into. Defining worthiness by health and fitness level is not just about size discrimination. It's also about classism. Racism. Ableism. And much more. Thanks to this new "beauty myth," far more people are unable to achieve not only the *body* that we say is acceptable, but also the *lifestyle* that we demand. It almost feels like we're looking at the most extreme form of elitism yet.

If we want to explore how extreme this beauty ideal has become, we need to look no further than a recently named eating disorder: orthorexia nervosa, also called "the health food eating disorder." Now before you roll your eyes or laugh at this term, let me explain what it means. When we call something a disorder, it's because we've crossed a line and that "thing" has started to affect our lives to the point where it's tremendously harmful. Eating an organic farm-to-table salad every day doesn't necessarily fall into disordered behaviors, but not being able to travel when you want to because you're worried about how clean the food will be? That may be. Limiting the types of foods you consume because it makes you feel good may not match the description, but feeling SO guilty for your "transgressions" when you don't follow your healthy eating rules that you spend the entire day loathing your existence? Maybe it's time to check in with yourself.

IMPORTANT SUMMARY: It's not the individual actions, but rather a pattern of obsession and the inability to function that becomes concerning. And understandably, these extreme behaviors are easy to adopt when you fully believe that your value, worth, and right to exist relies on how "healthy" you are.

Related to orthorexia is the fascinating term that professionals have started to use in conjunction with the trend of clean, raw, paleo, and health food movements: "righteous eating." This very clearly and automatically associates type of food with virtue, and even notes the religious tone now connected with what we consume. This, I feel, is a perfect example of how we, as a society, have become devout members of the Wellness Church.

Hallelujah and praise the Kale.

Overcoming and understanding this health/beauty myth was the last gigantic barrier in my path toward truly feeling good about my body. I learned to love my shape. My cellulite. My arms. My adult acne–ridden face. But I still found an unbearable amount of shame in all things health and fitness related. I was *terrified* to go to the doctor because they might tell me my cholesterol was too high and that I was now unhealthy. I had extreme shame about eating anything that wasn't "health food," especially in public. I would feel unsurmountable guilt if I missed a dance class (or four) and would internally berate myself for days. I would get embarrassed ordering a venti anything, even if I wanted it. I would try and hide my breathing when hiking up mountains or stairs. And the worst part was that I felt like there was no way out. I felt like the importance of health in relation to worthiness was inarguable and that it wasn't in any way unreasonable for others to expect me to obsess about it also.

I used to watch other fat activists post pictures of delicious s'mores and coffee that they found in a Bay Area café. Or write about a party they went to and how amazing the food was. Or mention how awesome pizza was in general. I was floored by their openness about their enjoyment of "unhealthy food" (and honestly, food in general), and, years into my activism, I still thought, "I could never do that." I thought they were *so brave*.

The reality? They know that our beauty ideal evolves with every standard we shatter. They realize that a new one arrives just as we find self-love in a new way. They get that the obsession with proving and glorifying health and fitness is just another way to regulate people and hinder self-esteem. Those activists weren't just brave. They were *smart*. Smart and onto the scam of obsessive health presented as a way to keep us all in line. I've got some serious RESPECT for those rad bitches.

Now, in addition to that focal point, other aspects of the original beauty ideal have shifted significantly in recent years. Namely, the subject of cisgender men and their body image issues. Naomi Wolf says in her updated introduction to *The Beauty Myth* that between 1990 and 2002 she watched the male body image market grow by leaps and bounds. Men are now increasingly targeted with anxiety-creating marketing formed around pure profit. "Men of all ages, economic backgrounds, and sexual orientations are more worried [about their appearance]— some a bit, others more substantially—than they were just ten years ago."[8] And this has continued to gain momentum since Wolf's update. In fact, since 2012, "beauty products" targeted at men have increased by 70 percent and men's "personal care" has become the fastest growing segment of the beauty industry—earning over four billion dollars in 2014.[9] This obsession with perfecting the male body isn't good by any means, but there is something else about this situation that REALLY concerns me. As women, we are now demanding and commandeering space to discuss and confront body images issues, and YAY, here's a book on it for chrissakes! But men? Because our culture now glorifies (white) strong, healthy, muscular, and "unbreakable" MEN, body pressure now affects them, too. But because of the focus on "manliness" and masculinity, guys are completely discouraged from talking about it.

Because women's economic and social power has increased over the years, men's old self-esteem standby of accumulating power and prestige through traditional and patriarchal means has started to diminish. This leaves men more vulnerable and in search of other ways to build confidence and worth. Cue men's health and fashion magazines, cosmetic surgery, Viagra sales, and, of course, eating disorders. Men are bullied, too. Men are taught to hate their midsections, too. Men are taught that they need to improve XYZ as well. But they are also told to "shake it off" and "man up" instead of addressing these traumatizing situations. Quite frankly, y'all, there is nothing more terrifying to me than complete silence when it comes to social injustice issues. Male body image issues may be "newly emerging" in comparison to the female beauty myth, but they are no less important than those of others. I can only hope that we as a society can work toward opening a safe space where these issues can be aired, processed, and then addressed.

It's really important to acknowledge that the beauty ideal will continue to evolve, change, and keep individuals imprisoned within their bodies for the foreseeable future. Say that we fight hard enough and normalize fat bodies. When/if we do, there will be another "you must become" that will sweep in and take its place. What this tells me is that believing that feeling "beautiful" (even our redefined version of it) can't be the totalistic goal of our body journey. The *start*? Sure! But not the end goal. We must also come to appreciate our bodies for what they are and do, come to peace with them as a whole, and love them so we can love others.

Now when I explain this to women, many are concerned about their urges to engage in traditional rituals that are directly connected to our "beauty ideal. They often ask me: "But what about wearing lipstick? Is that bad?"

Here's my personal opinion: We will always be influenced by the culture we grew up in. It's inevitable, and I don't think it's totally a bad thing. What's important is that we are conscious of this fact, cognizant of what that means, and aware that we have options outside of the norm. When we know these things, we are then able to make the very personal decision of what feels good to US.

There is a concept taught by a "professional tidier," named Marie Kondo, (yep, that's a thing) where she asks everyone to go through their houses and pick up each object. While holding each one, she challenges them, ask yourself one question along the lines of: *Does this bring me joy?* If the answer is yes, keep it. If no, discard it.

This also applies to the beauty standards we were raised with. I'm going to challenge you to mentally pick up each rule that you've been taught and ask yourself: *Does this bring me joy?*

For me? LIPSTICK BRINGS ME JOY. Especially the "fuck you" shades of red. Does dieting in pursuit of skinny bring me joy? No. It destroys my soul and will to live. Well, okay then. DISCARD. Dresses? Yes, so much joy. Tanning? No. Shaving my legs? Yes. Stilettos? No.

Your turn.

The most important thing is that you know how these beauty standards came about. That you know they were created by wealthy men in smoke-filled offices more than fifty years ago for monetary gain and control. That our hatred (which is fundamentally fear) of bodies that look different is *learned*. That the majority of photos are altered and impossible to achieve. That your level of engagement or disengagement in regard to "pretty" is up to you, and, no matter what you choose, it doesn't have any effect on your worthiness. That we have become so extreme in our adoption of "the beauty myth" we forget that we hate ourselves for not living up to a standard that does. Not. Exist.

Lord, help us all.

WEIGHTING TO BE SEEN: RACE,
INVISIBILITY, AND BODY POSITIVITY
SONYA RENEE TAYLOR OF THE BODY
IS NOT AN APOLOGY

My best friend Denise Jolly stood on a subway train and disrobed, revealing all 311 pounds of her formerly hidden body in a black bra and panties. This was the culmination of a thirty-day journey in which she took photos of herself in various states of partial nudity at home and in her community. She called it the Be Beautiful project. The extent of her nakedness in the photos was no more than what we might see on Victoria's Secret commercials or in beer ads, and yet it was revolutionary. In a society that tells us anyone with a body like hers is unworthy of being seen, let alone being loved, her work was a reminder to herself and others that "the active practice of loving myself exactly as I am is radical self-love." The photos were bold and powerful, and I asked her to capture her journey in an essay for The Body Is Not An Apology (TBINAA), a radical self-love and body-empowerment movement I founded four years ago.

The day after Denise's blog post was published, the story went viral. Denise was contacted by *The Huffington Post*, *Yahoo!*, *Inside Edition*, *The Queen Latifah Show*, *The Laura Ingraham Show*, and several other media outlets with requests to appear and give interviews. Her project achieved what it was supposed to: It made her seen. But when *The Huffington Post* re-posted her TBINAA, a slideshow of "body image heroes" was included—and nine white women's faces beamed at me with each click. The last woman pictured in the slideshow was Asian. If I am being honest, I felt the ugly tinge of jealousy creep up my spine when media outlets started calling me. After all, TBINAA started because of my choice to post a picture of my large body in just my undies on a social media page. I wondered, *Where was* The Huffington Post *then?* When I looked deeper at that ugly feeling it became clear it was not a personal jealousy about my gorgeous friend being seen in her brilliance. It was the bitter reminder of how often women of color, Black women specifically, are not seen.

The same day I watched the slideshow of body positive heroines, sans any Black or brown bodies, TBINAA posted a clip of *Glee*'s Amber Riley dominating the cha-cha-cha on *Dancing with the Stars*. There was nary a peep from the media about her beautiful example of movement, endurance, and power in a large body. Sure, several articles discussed what a great job she did. One even mentioned the fact that she was "plus-sized," but no one described television star Amber Riley as a body positive heroine. Why? Because the social narrative is, "She is a singing Black girl; she's supposed to be fat." That narrative renders her body an act of happenstance. Her body "just is," and therefore is not noteworthy. It would be like reporting that she has a nose. Of course she is fat, and her boldness in her particular body is nothing to aspire to.

Gabourey Sidibe, the breakout star of the 2009 film *Precious*, defied all odds and persevered beyond most of the entertainment industry's attempts to equate her with the illiterate food-addicted character she played in the film. Her out-loud, charismatic, ebullient personality and beauty continue to shine through, and yet she is not touted as a hero of body positivity. Her size and dark skin make her an outsider even in movements of inclusivity. Her absence from being included in any meaningful way in this dialogue is unsurprising but important. Black women have always found ways to live in our skin with a dignity the world has not afforded us. When Black women's bodies are acknowledged, it is usually to pathologize them. A Google search of "Black women" and "body image" leads to scores of Internet hits on the "obesity crisis" in Black communities. When the word "Black" is removed, the same search generates article upon article of white women embracing body positivity.

In Western culture, white womanhood is held up as the epitome of beauty and desire. Part of the machine of size discrimination is stripping white women of that status as punishment for fatness. There is a way in which body positive movements both reject the notion of the body as object while reclaiming it as beautiful by dismantling the definition. Black women's bodies have always been objects in the social sphere, but are never exalted as beautiful. The fat Black woman's body has been rendered as an object of service, whether for food, advice, care-taking, or other areas, but it has never been something to aspire to, not a thing of beauty. The mammy, a stereotypical trope born out of slavery, validated large Black women's existence only through their service to white women and white families. Think *Gone with the Wind*, the 1980s television show *Gimme a Break*, or the film adapted from the book *The Help*. Our society tells us fatness is not beautiful. Blackness is not beautiful. So, even while as a society we may be starting to reclaim size diversity as beautiful, the presence of Blackness complicates the narrative. We don't deal well with complications, which often means we don't deal with complications at all, particularly in the realm of race. We simply don't tell those stories. It is this unwillingness to wade through the murky waters of race that make Black and brown women invisible even in the places where we say we are trying to make people seen.

There are reasons women like Stella Boonshoft and Denise Jolly's images have gone viral. Without question a great deal of that is about their brave declarations of beauty about their bodies, bodies that the world says should not be seen as such. However, their loud demands for a seat at the table must be mitigated by the reality that, as white women, they at least have always been *invited* to the table so long as they could fit into the prescribed seat. This is a birthright women of color have never had. What I thought was jealousy about a friend's success was not that at all; what I was feeling was the aching reminder that the vehicle to even beginning to dismantle weight stigma in order to be seen as fully human in this society is, far too often, a privilege that requires white skin. No matter how much I weigh or how naked I get, I will never have that.

*

if you're happy and you know it, cut in line: fat hate isn't your problem

While I was writing this book, a radical thing happened. Something SO BIG it broke the entire Internet: Plus-size model Tess Holliday rocked people's worlds by becoming the first model "of her size" to be signed to an agency. Her size: 5'5" and a size 22—a far cry from the industry's standard of size-10 hourglass-y figures. Plus-size models *never wear above a size 16/18*, and are usually 5'8" or taller. Guys . . . Tess is super short and super fat and breaking all the mother-fucking rules like the *super*hero she is.

GOD I WAS EXCITED.

But changing the status quo is *anything* but easy. If I ever want to mourn humanity, all I have to do is scroll through the comments on Tess's Instagram. Kids, don't try this at home. Just let me tell you what you'll find so you don't have to mourn humanity, too. It's a rare prac-tice for me, but when I DO take a second to remind myself that body activism is important by looking through her account, I find hundreds upon hundreds (collectively, thousands . . . we might be up to millions) of comments in which people call her barnyard animal names, spout "facts" about how she'll die early because: science, or express their concern about the fact that she's a negative role model for promoting obesity by loving herself . . . and those are the kind ones.

But let's distract ourselves for a second and recognize that Tess has been covered positively by so many major publications it leaves *this* gal in awe. *Time* magazine, the cover of *People*, *Cosmopolitan*, *CNN*, *Nylon* magazine, *TMZ*, the *Daily Mail*, *Life & Style*, and dozens (and dozens) of others. For a few days after the announcement that Tess was signed to a modeling agency, if you were to look at your Facebook sidebar you'd see her name trending. The fact that this woman's sexy mug was on every website during that time was revolutionary, and I enjoyed every second of it.

But even that positive press attracted judgmental opinions and nasty comments. Tess is not the only one who regularly receives a monstrous amount of blatant hate and criticism; I am presented with my fair share of cruel words, and so are most of the bloggers and advocates I know. And sadly, this is not just limited to well-known personalities. The #fatkini hashtag (which is used as a tag on plus bikini photos) was attacked on Instagram not too long ago, and hateful comments were left for everyday users who posted a picture with the empowering tag.

For years, this vitriol has left me puzzled and asking: WHY is this happening? WHY is loving yourself so controversial? WHY U SO MAD, WORLD?

Well, I've since learned why, and I'm gonna tell you all about it, goddamnit! The explanation is as multifaceted as they come, but I'll share with you **three significant reasons** for the confounding weight hate we see online and in real life. Not only is this information fascinating in a know-your-enemies kind of way, but it also gives us a starting point for our personal understanding—which is critical if we're going to ignore the hate and continue on our awesome way.

#3: RIDE A BIKE.

I'm not even going to dignify the idea that fat people shouldn't ride bikes by speculating as to why that might be. Instead, I'm just going to talk about how much I love Tucson, and bike riding. Guys, I fucking love both of these things a lot.

I used to ride a bicycle everywhere, and didn't even have a car for years. So fuck you, haters. I love bicycle riding more than I love a lot of things, and I'm not quitting anytime soon.

Oh yeah. And I totally ride bicycles in miniskirts. No big deal.

Your challenge: Rent a bike from a bike shop or bike-share program in your city, buy your own, or dust off that old two-wheeler from the past. Strap on a helmet and get riding!

1. Body Currency

This is the issue that strikes me the hardest. This, along with learning the historical events behind body hate, completely transformed the way I see body image issues and politics. In short: THE CONCEPT OF BODY CURRENCY BLEW MY MIND, Y'ALL.

Body currency goes something like this: We as a society are taught that IF we achieve the ideal body that we see in traditional media (and not before), our work will then be rewarded with everything we desire: love, worthiness, success, and ultimately happiness. Which is what we all want, right?

Because the vast majority of our culture buys into this, we have millions upon millions of people **investing everything they have** into achieving the ultimate goal: thinness, which *obviously* equals happiness, remember? (Other body "goals" also apply here, like able-bodied/

light skin color/cisgender appearance, and so on.) SO, people spend their lives in a perpetual state of self-loathing (which we sadly call "inspiration"!) while working their asses off to become that ideal. We Americans sink billions of dollars into beauty products every year, and we gift the weight-loss industry over *$60 billion.*[1] Fourteen million of us had cosmetic procedures in 2012, and yes, that number keeps growing.[2] Perhaps we starve ourselves or maybe we just fixate on our calorie count like it will determine our salvation. Maybe we make the gym our god. Whatever we choose individually, we as a country have made "fixing our bodies" our main obsession, and we let it consume our lives. This is the case for most of us, whether we choose to acknowledge it or not. We live to give our all to the quest toward impossible perfection (marketed as happiness).

So THEN, after all of this, when a fat chick who *hasn't* done the work, who *hasn't* "paid the price" by trying to fix her body, who *doesn't* have any interest in the gospel we so zealously believe in, *stands up and says*: I'M HAPPY! . . . we freak the fuck out.

Because: That bitch just broke the rules. She just cut in front of us in line. She just unwittingly ripped us off. And she essentially made our lifetime of work totally meaningless.

It's kind of like investing everything you have into some sort of stock, and instead of its worth increasing you're notified that its value is now the same as Monopoly money. Suddenly, your investments (a.k.a. "body currency") have the devastating value of **zero**.

I've been there, and I was pissed too.

The obvious problem with body currency is that thinness doesn't necessarily equal happiness. Remember the last chapter? Our thinness quest just equals money in the pockets of companies who sell us insecurity to make sure that we're repeat customers. It's a real shitty move on their part, and leaves anyone who believes in the scam SOL, which then makes them angry without really knowing why. *So* they direct all their anger toward those who cheated the system and found the pot of gold (happiness) without doing *any* of the goddamn work.

Tess is the perfect target for this sort of anger and fat hate: She's successful (Italian *Vogue*, y'all), she's in love (he's darling *and* has an Australian accent), she publicly shares that she believes she's worthy, and . . . goddamnit, she's fucking happy. All while being very much NOT thin, and NOT in any way working toward becoming thin.

THE NERVE! Amiright?

In a killer interview with *Yahoo! Shine*, Virgie Tovar recaps it ever so eloquently (as she often tends to do):

> *"Fat" is just the current catchall word for all the things that we as a culture are afraid of: women's rights, people refusing to acquiesce to cultural pressures of conformity, fear of mortality. [People who hate fat people] see body love as a move toward people taking charge of their lives and choosing what they want to do, no matter what the culture says. This is really scary to a lot of people. The anger they express is actually toward themselves. A person who hates seeing a happy, liberated person wishes they had the strength to do that, but they are too entrenched or "bought in" to the way things are right now to see it as a beautiful thing. So they see it and they hate it . . . People have invested a lot of time and a lot of resources into this game that says "thin wins." So when people see exceptions to that rule, they feel personally invalidated, personally stolen from, personally affronted."[3]*

If you haven't listened to the episode of *This American Life* called, "If You Don't Have Anything Nice to Say, SAY IT IN ALL CAPS," I'd recommend you do. Within this illuminating episode, Lindy West shares her constant run-ins with Internet hate and recounts an *unheard-of* instance where a particularly vile "troll" emailed her with a genuine *apology*.

It totally happened, so pick your jaw up off the floor already.

Because this girl ain't got no fear, Lindy called him up to talk about why he hated her so much. After asking him why he chose *her* of all people to torment, the interview went something like this:

> **Man:** *Well, it revolved around one issue that you wrote about a lot which was your being heavy—the struggles that you had regarding being a woman of size, or whatever the term may be.*
>
> **Lindy West:** *You can say fat. That's what I say. . . .*
>
> **Man:** *Fat. OK, fat. When you talked about being proud of who you are and where you are and where you're going, that kind of stoked that anger that I had.*

The man shared that he was done with Internet harassment nowadays, but confessed that during the time that he lashed out at Lindy, he was living what he called a "passionless life." That he hated his body, had been dumped, and worked at a job he despised. He had the opposite of happiness.

The interesting thing is that since then he's started school again, found a girlfriend, started teaching little kids, and found fulfillment. He also no longer tries to inflict pain on others online. It's fascinating how this works. It just goes to show what everyone has known all along: **Happy people don't try to purposely hurt other people.**

I mean, this isn't a well-kept secret, not by a long shot. You might even go so far as to assume this is common knowledge (and as indisputable as Ira Glass's example of the gray boxes in the podcast—OMG, go listen to the beginning, it's hilarious), but you'd be surprised at the number of people who argue this simple concept.[4] For example, one comment on a Prince Ea video about haters and their anger made me giggle: "I post a few vulgar comments . . . and people auto assume I'm some unhappy asshole in real life. How about people stop being so goddamn sensitive?"[5]

Someone please give this guy a hug.

This concept applies to our appearance as well: **People who love their bodies don't try to purposely make other people hate their own.**

Or as Meghan Tonjes puts it: "People who disrespect the bodies of others really don't think that much of their own. I promise."[6]

Unfortunately, *it's no wonder* we see hostility online. Why? Because so many in our country (and beyond) spend their time tirelessly attempting to run toward an empty dream. Because body currency is a frustrating farce. Because all of those people have learned to hate their current bodies, and most have *no idea* that they can think differently. But the fact of the matter is, you can. Body love isn't just for fat people, it's for every person imaginable. Everyone has the right to self-love. Skinny people. Fat people. Short people. Tall people. All abilities. All sizes. All shapes. All shades. All sexes. All genders. Haters and lovers alike.

After all, we're all in this bullshit together. Throughout my "travels" online and IRL, I have yet to meet a woman who doesn't have something she'd like to change about her body, and men are in a similar boat except they're absolutely *forbidden* to talk about it. We've all been fed the same lies, and while that doesn't give *anyone* the right to purposely hurt others, it does give us that crucial starting point for understanding.

2. Institutionalized Sexism

While "the race to thin" plays a huge and significant role in the negativity that is thrown toward body-lovin' peeps, there are also other factors at play, one of those being sexism that is heavily institutionalized. Yes, ma'am. And while this will definitely garner a few eye rolls, some body hate has a lot to do with a favorite word of *those scary feminists*: patriarchy.

That interview on *This American Life* continues:

> **Lindy West:** *OK, so you found my writing. You found my writing, and you did not like it.*

> **Man:** *Certain aspects of it.... You used a lot of all caps. You're just a very—you almost have no fear when you write. . . . You know, it's like you stand on the desk and you say, I'm Lindy West, and this is what I believe in. Fuck you if you don't agree with me. And even though you don't say those words exactly, I'm like, who is this bitch who thinks she knows everything?*

Lindy then questioned whether the reason for these strong feelings might be because she's a woman.

> **Man:** *Oh, definitely. Definitely. Women are being more forthright in their writing. There isn't a sense of timidity to when they speak or when they write. They're saying it loud. And I think that—and I think, for me, as well, it's threatening at first.*[7]

This may have been a phone call with one man, but his opinions are ubiquitous. We hate watching women step out of line, speak up, and take up space. It instigates the fear Virgie talked about, which comes from not being able to control others, from not having the organized complacency that we need so desperately to feel safe. Paulo Freire said it best in one sentence: "Functionally, oppression is domesticating."[8] Oppression certainly serves its purpose—it makes outspoken and confident women a threat to our comfortable system. Which means that outspoken and confident women who are also FAT? Well, they're another rule-breaking satanic breed altogether.

As women, we are disproportionately taught that our physical appearance is what makes us valuable, and that we must work toward becoming the perfect example of beauty in order to be worthwhile. As noted in many feminist texts, this includes taking up as little space as possible—not only physically, but emotionally, verbally, and on every other front as well.

In one Facebook conversation, some friends and I noted how it's the fierce fatties that threaten everyone's paradigm; not necessarily those who are fat and apologetic. Gabi Gregg of *Gabifresh.com* (and the one who started the fatkini photo trend) nailed it when she said: "If there is a fat person on television trying super hard to lose weight, crying about how hard life is, and talking about how they eat to cope etc., then everyone is at home crying and cheering them on. Put that same person in a crop top while they smile, and the pitchforks come out."[9]

Preach, girl.

If a fat woman buys into the same mumbo jumbo as everyone else, we might feel empathy for her. We're ALL for her working toward her goal, just like us. Or maybe we just allow her to exist without acknowledgment until she has become our version of desirable. But if she shows any glimmer of happiness, self-esteem, or success without following the commandments? Well then, off with her head, and LET'S TELEVISE IT!

Fat women who deliberately take up space, speak out, and achieve the happiness we all desire are the perfect trifecta of terror. They represent a terror that we can't control, and so we throw our hate at them by the handful in hopes that they quiet down, shut up, and get back in line.

Jesus Christ, we've got so far to go.

3. Limited Media Representation

Another reason we find ourselves "in hate" with fat people has to do a lot with how they are represented (and are NOT represented) in the media. When fat bodies *do* appear (significantly less often than slender bodies do) in television shows, movies, political comics, literature, and animation, they are consciously presented in highly curated ways, all of which are meant to initiate knee-jerk reactions. They give us a limited way of processing fat people and none of the presentations are particularly positive.

Lindsey Averill, co-producer of *Fattitude: A Body Positive Documentary,* has done extensive research regarding the problematic portrayal of fat figures in pop culture. She shared her findings in an interview with *Refinery 29*: "There are 10 to 15 archetypes for fat characters. But, they tend to be problematic, meaning outside the normal sphere of culture. Fat characters don't have average experiences or stories. They don't have their own stories at all. They're the subplot."[10]

These canned archetypes are not actual people, like Melissa McCarthy (for example), but rather characters Melissa McCarthy *plays*. The fat archetype can range from the Best Friend, to the Hypersexual or the Asexual (as Averill mentions), to the Slovenly Roommate and beyond, but there are three very general fat person tropes that I personally find to be very present and harmful: the Stupid Fat Person, the Funny Fat Person, and the Evil Fat Person. Allow me to illustrate:

- **The Stupid Fat Person:** One of my favorite examples of this character is perfectly demonstrated through the comedy duo Abbott and Costello. There is a thin person and a fat person . . . and when it comes down to intelligence, guess who's the idiot? You guessed it! Other examples of stupid fat characters include Patrick Star from *SpongeBob SquarePants*, Peter Griffin from *Family Guy*, Curly from *The Three Stooges*, Augustus Gloop from *Charlie and the Chocolate Factory*, Dudley from *Harry Potter*, Eric Cartman from *South Park*, and Homer Simpson of *The Simpsons*. Nodding your head yet?

- **The Funny Fat Person:** Oh, how we *love* to laugh at fat people. Thousands of memes have been created just for this form of entertainment. Comedians often play off of this archetype, something found in even the earliest comics. A perfect example of the funny fat archetype can be found in another classic duo: Laurel and Hardy. One thin, one fat. The fat guy often becomes the main butt of the jokes. Other fat and funny characters include Fat Bastard from *Austin Powers*, Chunk from *The Goonies*, Harold from *Hey Arnold*, Peter and Meg from *Family Guy* (many MANY fat characters appear in multiple categories), Mikey from *Recess*, Eric Cartman from *South Park*, Homer Simpson of *The Simpsons*, and Miss Piggy from *The Muppet Show*.

* **The Evil Fat Person:** And last but certainly not least is our evil fat villain. Some of these characters provoke moral outrage, some laughs, and others sheer disgust. It's always easy to hate the nefarious fat person: Ursula from *The Little Mermaid*, Penguin from *Batman*, Slug from Marvel Comics, the Queen of Hearts from *Alice in Wonderland*, Oogie Boogie from *The Nightmare Before Christmas*, Big Dan Teague from *O Brother, Where Art Thou?*, Eric Cartman from *South Park* (the trifecta!), countless mob bosses, fat cats, and of course, the most gluttonous of them all, Jabba the Hut.

It's important to note that not all stupid, funny, and evil characters are fat; many are thin or fall somewhere in between. What is problematic is when we see fat characters, they fall into these negative stereotypes more often than not.

Thanks to these common and prevailing tropes, we are repulsed/ humored/angered by fat people because our reality has no other frame of reference in which to sort them out. For the most part they are not positively represented in the media, so when we see fat people happy, in love, feeling worthy, achieving success, or engaging in any positive activity . . . our brains break. A FAT PERSON WHO ISN'T MISERABLE OR TRYING TO BECOME UN-FAT? *We don't know how to process this information.* We don't understand. The unfamiliarity is uncomfortable. We feel confused . . . and this often leads to mockery, anger, and yes, hate.

One of my FAVORITE (sarcasm) things I've run across on the Internet comes from the University of Connecticut Rudd Center for Food Policy and Obesity (uconnruddcenter.org). The Rudd Center focused on "reducing weight stigma" within journalistic coverage. This gallery, created to "humanize" fat bodies, contains 451 images of fatties doing elementary exercise (they can do wha?); gardening, shopping for, and cooking raw fruits and vegetables (how *healthy* of you, fat people!); wearing business casual clothing; and talking on cell phones (they hold jobs too!); and three images of a fat couple holding hands.

While I appreciate that the Rudd Center is *attempting* to change the lens in which the world views fat people, not much is solved by encouraging the use of images that show fat people doing mostly things that are supposedly going to make them less fat, which has always been the ultimate goal. Do you see where I'm coming from here? I'm SO glad to *not* see the kind of degrading "headless fatty" images that are ubiquitous among stock photo galleries and other corners of the Internet, or pictures of fat people crying while holding their love handles. But even those who are committed to portraying fat people in a positive light have galleries where the majority of images shows them in the same tired and insensitive way. Instead of those 451 images of fat bodies doing limited activities, I want to see fat people holding hands with lovers of all sizes, enjoying coffee with friends, smiling, and maybe even one à la Julie Andrews singing in the fields and spinning while singing at the top of her lungs. You know, fat people doing a range of normal happy things, like they very often do.

The majority of society isn't capable of producing these images yet, but guess what? We are.

A simple way to start to change the way fatties are represented is to take the narrative into our own hands and show the world what's actually real. We can take our own unscripted images and share them all over the Internet—a tactic similar to "culture jamming," and an effective technique for countering fucked-up societal standards. BUT, if we want to do something a little simpler, we can just live a visible and unapologetic life cram-packed with fulfillment, happiness, and joy. All of these things challenge the warped versions of fat that our world sees and offer those around us a new paradigm in which to process larger bodies.

It's really that straightforward, and eventually we'll get there. I'm hoping the rest of the world will join us soon.

Until then, haters will continue to say whatever they feel about Tess and every fat person they consider to be a poor role model. They'll continue to be unaware of why they feel jilted by the body currency exchange. They'll continue to try and keep loud women in line and tell them to behave. They'll continue to portray large bodies as the comfortable tropes they know so well. They'll continue to live incognizant of why they are outraged by others being happy and blind to the reasons why they hate fat people SO much. But who knows? Maybe some will wise up. And though I wouldn't put money down on a sweeping change in the majority (because we're just not there yet), there are people working on a societal transformation, and we're making some progress. Remember Tess's success? Being the first super fat chick to sign with a London modeling agency and all? That's progress, my friends.

> **For those of you facing any kind of body hate, do me a favor: Ignore those people who tell you loving yourself is not okay.**

For those of you facing any kind of body hate, do me a favor: Ignore those people who tell you loving yourself is not okay. Have empathy for the people that hate you for being happy; we all know what that kind of self-loathing feels like. It's not required, but if you can, send them body-lovin' vibes, because they deserve to love their whole selves too. Acknowledge that the people spreading the animosity are simply regurgitating deception that's been fed to our culture for decades; they just don't know anything different. So keep on rockin' your version of your bad self, and in the words of Tess, don't forget to "surround yourself with positive, like-minded people who support you. It's crucial to your happiness and well-being. Never compare yourself to others and celebrate what makes you, YOU."[11]

And if you ever find yourself struggling and can't seem to shake the motherfucking hate (it gets REAL sometimes), I offer you this "life well lived" Twitter wisdom from Gabourey Sidibe, star of the film *Precious*, as inspiration:

> @GabbySidibe: *To people making mean comments about my GG pics, I mos def cried about it on that private jet on my way to my dream job last night. #JK*

Find your own version of a dream job. Find your own version of a private jet. Your fat body is not a hindrance, and it's *certainly* not a barrier to happiness. The only barrier is the false belief that you must change yourself in order to be okay. You've got the power to shake the bullshit, trust me.

Now go get happy, kick some ass, and LIVE already.

HE SAID I'M GETTING FAT
ANDREW WALEN, LCSW-C OF
THE BODY IMAGE THERAPY CENTER

When I was about ten years old, my step-grandmother was married to a lout of a man. I mean, he was a real schmuck. He didn't like people and didn't want to be bothered by his wife's new extended family (that's where I came in). When I came into his den to say hello during a visit, he looked at my pudgy little boy belly and said to me, "Andy, you're getting fat!" He then farted in my direction.

This vile man managed in that one quick encounter to engage my already shaky sense of self and help fuel my self-loathing. And I let him. Experiences like this were cumulative, every little moment of fat-shaming building and coalescing into an eating-disorder voice that drove me to countless diets, exercise binges, food binges, starvations, and bulimic behaviors. It took years of therapy and nutrition counseling, social and family support, and learning to value myself beyond my body size and shape to silence that eating-disorder voice.

On the first day of this new year, I was visiting my father when a friend of his popped in. This man looked at me and said, "Andy, you've really grown! I mean you've really put on some pounds!" Are you kidding me? I'm a forty-two-year-old man now, and still this *alter cocker* thinks it's okay to fat-shame me? Hell. No!

I did not disrespect my father by yelling at his friend, and I did not lose my cool. I've taught my family over the years that I will not tolerate fat-shaming, weight prejudice, or diet talk at all. I can't help it if they're still surrounded by folks who, like them, never learned to see this as destructive as it is. But I also learned how to thicken my skin and not let insensitive comments like this get to me anymore. I don't let it shake my foundation of recovery and instead see it for what it is: ignorance. I'm fully aware of my gifts, my attributes, my sources of confidence and pride. I'm not thin, haven't been since age five. I live in a bigger body and that's just my body, it's not who I am as a father, husband, therapist, friend, son, or any other identity I have.

What can you do when you're faced with a similar situation? I recommend following an anger roadmap. First off, recognize you're upset and breathe for a second. When you're able to think clearly, then go ahead and follow these steps. First off, was the comment made maliciously, with intent to harm? If yes, then it deserves further attention. If not done intentionally, then you really want to consider whether it deserves your time and attention. If you say yes, then examine whether you have a reasonable response. By this I mean, can you effect some change by confronting the person—talk to them, teach them, help them see how they hurt you and others by this kind of comment? If you don't think they'll hear you, then by engaging this person all you're doing is escalating the situation. That helps no one, including you. You then can decide to do what I did, which is talk yourself through it and focus on challenging the eating-disorder beliefs the comment has started up in your brain. Dispute the thought of decrepitude, and then move on to the next task at hand. It's okay to be angry, but don't let it become a replacement for your eating-disorder voice. Ultimately, the voice of love and respect is the one that will sustain you.

But it's not easy. I get it. To be a man and struggle with body image issues, weight discrimination, and eating-disorder behaviors is to feel like an outcast. Men are supposed to be strong, dominant, and competitive, and not need external help. That cultural expectation leads to men shying away from any mental health care, let alone for an issue that is supposedly a "female" one. But we're affected by the change in expectations for our bodies. You won't find very many pictures of men with average bodies in magazines, just the extremes of the "overweight," whom we shame, and the "well-built," whom we celebrate. Decades ago, researchers found only a small percentage of males felt uncomfortable with their bodies. Now that number is closer to 90 percent, half wishing they were bigger and half wishing they were smaller. All wish they had more muscle definition, and are especially concerned with how their bodies look from the waist up. It's about the six-pack abs, V-shaped torso, striations in the musculature, and round-ness of the biceps, triceps, and deltoids.

And what is often seen in the gyms? Men who come in for hours at a time, working on their "show-off" muscles in their arms, legs, and abs, paying little attention to overall strength and balance. This is usually followed by burning out on cardio machines so they can "eat whatever the hell I want." Where's the balance? Why so much focus on looks? Because we are in denial about our insecurities in life, love, work, rela-tionships, family, and the like. We control what we can on our own, don't talk about our feelings, don't ask for help, don't show weakness, "man up!" That's the rule. That's the norm. And it's a damn shame.

Many women I speak with believe only gay men struggle with body image and eating disorders. Truth is, only about 15 percent of males with eating disorders are gay.[1] That leaves millions of straight men with eating disorders and body image issues. Unfortunately, research doesn't support this issue either, as only a minuscule percent-age focuses on males with eating disorders.

We have to do better. We have to normalize the experience of men with body image and eating-disorder concerns. We have to say that being a man means facing our fears about intimacy, vulnerability, and connection. "Manning up" would take on a whole new connota-tion. And maybe, just maybe, nobody else will attempt to shame me by calling me fat.

*

fat and health: rethink that shit

[CHAPTER FIVE]

Let me start out by blowing your mind with four very simple statements:

- Skinny bodies can be unhealthy.
- Fat bodies can be unhealthy.
- Skinny bodies can be healthy.
- And fat bodies *can* be healthy.

Yes. These are all true, and there are real, live, existing bodies that prove it everywhere.

What do those four very simple statements mean? Fat bodies aren't inherently unhealthy, and skinny bodies aren't inherently healthy. That's a far cry from the FAT = BAD and SKINNY = GOOD paradigm we've been raised to think of as gospel. It also means we have to remove weight from the health equation and look at other signifiers of health. It also means a lot of mean people are sad that they can't play the role of Doctor and Concerned Citizen while judging people's state of health just by looking at them. *God*, I'm such a downer.

It's actually a documented fact that being fat isn't an indicator of being unhealthy, and being thin is no assurance of good health.[1] But you'd never believe it based on diet, health, and weight-loss ads. Just a reminder, dear friends: This is a fundamental truth.

I'm NOT saying that everyone walking around the world is in perfect health no matter their body size (not that perfect health is a prerequisite for loving ourselves; more on that later). I'm also not saying every skinny lady is unhealthy and every fat woman is a healthful goddess. What I AM saying is weight is NOT the health determinant that we so desperately want it to be. I'm saying that weight is not the number-one way to diagnose a person's "wellness." I'm saying that judging a person's worth based on her body is fucked up, especially when it comes to health. HAVE I BELABORED THIS POINT ENOUGH?

Good.

Some people may tell you this is bullshit. Professionals who clinically study and disprove common health myths (like fat = bad) often talk about how they can present pages and pages of scientific studies that show our assumption of weight and health isn't what we think it is, and this still doesn't change people's bias. We are SO invested in and bombarded by the idea that thin means fit and fat means death that for some, updating their mindset is seemingly impossible. And let's be real: There is a lot of money being spent to ensure this continues. There's a really good chance some of you will walk away from this chapter assuming that I hit my head too many times as a child, and y'know what? That's okay. This is your life and your rules, and you get to decide what you believe. But if you find yourself teetering and feeling like you're just not quite able to let go of ingrained body morals, but you kinda want to, I'm going to share a few truths that don't have anything to do with blood pressure or treadmills: Self-esteem isn't a crime. Self-love isn't something to be earned. Most importantly, loving your fat body as it is *is not* delusional and *does not* amount to self-deception.

But believing that you are less of a person just because greedy assholes said so? I propose that *is,* and *does.*

The majority of opinions about fat people and health still fall into two general camps that go something like: (1) *Fat isn't healthy, you Obeast!* and (2) *You may not need to be a size 2, just be healthy and fit* (cue our new worth indicator from Chapter 3, remember?). We've covered multiple reasons that both of these camps are so prevalent. Now let's talk about the connection between our obsession with health and our belief that all doctors are reliable consultants when it comes to defining this important factor. Because the world believes the "obesity crisis" is going to cause an apocalypse (and the only way to survive is by working out every day and eating shit tons of carrots), we need to question the mouthpieces that most people refuse to contest and ask ourselves: Where is this definition of health coming from, and is it accurate?

In short? It comes from people who are as susceptible to bias as the rest of us, so not really.

In 2013, hundreds of doctors gathered at the annual meeting of the American Medical Association to vote on organizational policies. One of the policies up for a vote was a particularly brief resolution: "That our American Medical Association recognize obesity as a disease state with multiple pathophysiological aspects requiring a range of interventions to advance obesity treatment and prevention." Even though many AMA professionals already know what we do—that fat bodies aren't always unhealthy—it passed anyway. This was followed shortly thereafter (this year, 2015) with a new guideline for all medical staff: Treat the weight first.[2]

Now, of course, like every industry that's ever existed, monetary gain is always a key motive. There is a lot of money to be made by "treating" fat people in general, and there are compensations as a result of that 2013 decision: Now that obesity is officially a "disease," doctors can write the diagnosis on their chart and get compensated by insurance companies. Fact. Is unbiased health always the priority for medical professionals? No fucking way.

"It sounds like you're saying fat people are victims of some sort of medical conspiracy. GOD, YOU SOUND SO DRAMATIC, JES." Nah. I'm just presenting the facts. I'll let you decide.

Now, is every fatty who shows up at the doctor going to have a clean bill of health and have no weight-related issues? No. Will some people benefit from weight treatment? It totally depends on what *they* believe is best for *them*. Should we discredit everything that comes out of a doctor's mouth? Not necessarily, but let's at least ask questions. Is weight the only contributing factor to health issues? Nope. Does our medical system operate under this premise? Fuck no.

Now, when fat people *do* have medical issues (and use those tax dollars everyone likes to bitch and moan about), it's important to think about why it can happen since we know it's not *always* because of weight. There are two particular issues that I feel are especially relevant that *don't* draw a direct line to the scale.

1. Dieting

Tell me what the cause of this list of symptoms sounds like to you: "Increased all-cause mortality and . . . increased mortality from cardiovascular disease. . . . Increased risk for myocardial infarction, stroke, and diabetes, increased high-density lipoprotein cholesterol, increased systolic and diastolic blood pressure, and even suppressed immune function."[3]

Sounds an awful lot like what we get all shamey about and pin onto fat bodies, doesn't it? Well I'll tell ya what: It's not a list of risks correlated with "obesity," but rather those that come from weight cycling, or as we often call it: yo-yo dieting

Guys, it's a well-known fact that diets don't work, and this means that every diet is pretty much a yo-yo diet.

I'm sorry if that ruined your day. There's a shit ton of research that talks about this. One well-known and still relevant statistic is that 95 percent of people who diet will gain the weight back within three to five years, and it's very common that they gain more than was lost (for more on this, do an online search for "Ragen Chastain Do 95% of Dieters Really Fail?").[4]

Those symptoms listed above? Pretty rotten side effects that severely impact a person's health. I find it SO odd that we have decided to shame large bodies without knowing anything about their health, and then applaud anyone who diets when doing so can be physically harmful in a big way (and costs tax dollars, too). We treat fatness like it is always a death sentence (it's not) while encouraging every person to "better themselves" by dieting, which in fact causes its own list of ailments. It's backwards as fuck, y'all.

If we were REALLY concerned about someone else's health we wouldn't emphatically encourage dieting like we do. Seeing that 75 percent of women have disordered eating,[5] 116 million American adults are dieting at any given time,[6] and 80 percent of ten-year-olds have already started dieting,[7] I'd say it's time we stop congratulating others for harming their bodies in pursuit of fabricated perfection. Let's start there.

2. Aversion to Health Care Because: Goddamn Discrimination

Weight-biased health care isn't anything new. We like to assume the medical professionals we come in contact with are honest, nonpartisan, and well . . . professional. This is not always the case. There is a boat load of documentation that explores how these professionals feel about fatties, and it's not very awesome.

It's been heavily documented that doctors share the same high level of intolerance and disgust of fat bodies as the general population. One study showed that over 50 percent of primary care physicians viewed fat patients as "awkward," "unattractive," and "noncompliant." A third of these physicians described fat patients as "weak-willed," "sloppy," and "lazy."[8] In another study, 45 percent of a sample of physicians agreed they have a negative reaction to fat individuals.[9] It is so common for fatties to go to doctor's appointments with a particular non-weight-related issue and leave with a prescription that will "help" them lose that weight. One hilarious (darkly so) cartoon illustrates this concept: A fat woman with a wooden post stuck through her midsection says, "DOCTOR! I've been impaled!" to which the doctor responds, "Well, maybe you'd feel better if you lost some weight."[10] I wish this were an uncommon response to serious medical issues, but unfortunately it's not. Blogs like *First, Do No Harm* ("Real Stories of Fat Prejudice in Health Care," at www.fathealth.wordpress.com), are chock full of stories of experiences people have had with weight discrimination in the medical field. It will make you cringe.

Even further, a recent government survey indicated that more than half of the "overweight" adults being told they are unhealthy by doctors are metabolically healthy, and nearly one in four "normal-weight," metabolically unhealthy adults are overlooked by doctors.[11] So a majority of fat people are being told they're not okay when they are, and "straight-size" bodies are automatically assumed to be up to snuff and don't recieve proper medical attention. This simply goes to show that medical weight bias negatively affects us all.

All of this, understandably, can make fat people really hate going to the doctor. So much so that they often don't. And I DON'T FUCKING BLAME THEM. Not only is so much of our worth attached to our "health" and what the doctors say, there's more than a 50 percent chance that the mouthpiece of that info is gonna be a dick. Fat people are surrounded by judgmental dicks all day long. We certainly don't want to pay to see one. Y'KNOW?

Of course you know.

As a general rule, avoiding doctor's visits isn't the best thing, and can, of course, lead to other (yep, costly) ailments. Fatness itself isn't the health issue we think it is, but our *hatred* of fat plays a larger role than we ever bother to acknowledge. Period.

"Jes, this is kind of long and boring and is making me really sad.

Why are you sharing this with me?" I know. I'm getting frustrated and cynical just typing it. But I'm sharing this with you because these are the trusted professionals we all rely on. And you know what? Some of the practitioners mentioned above *are* well intentioned and see themselves as caring and compassionate! But the issue remains that even though they may have been trained to believe that perpetuating these weight-related myths is helpful, many are still people with documented bias. While they may not *mean* harm, entrenched stigma can and does hurt patients of all sizes. Feel free to take all this information as you will. I just want to make sure you know what the fuck is going on in this realm so you can make decisions that are best for you.

So what DO we do then, now that this bullshit indicator of health called weight is defunct? Well, many body advocates like to turn to a little thing called Health at Every Size (HAES)*.

One of the amazing humans behind this epic, clinically based movement and author of the book *Health at Any Size: The Surprising Truth About Your Weight*, is Linda Bacon, PhD. If you have any further questions about HAES after reading this chapter (you will), I recommend you pick it up. In it, Dr. Bacon debunks some of the most pernicious myths: The only way for obese people to improve health is to lose weight, anyone who is determined can lose weight and keep it off through diet and exercise, fat is costly, and adiposity poses a significant morbidity risk.

"But Jes, HAES is obviously all about health, too. AREN'T YOU CONTRADICTING YOURSELF?" Patience, grasshopper.

The HAES website, www.healthateverysize.com, states, "**Health at Every Size is the new peace movement.** Very simply, it acknowledges that good health can best be realized independent from considerations of size. It supports people of all sizes in addressing health directly by adopting healthy behaviors."

The goal of HAES isn't to increase your worth; they know you're already worthy. It isn't to get you to become the slim and fit ideal; they recognize that naturally diverse bodies exist. It isn't to make you a superior human being; that's just silly. **HAES simply teaches**

the concept of treating your body "well" because you love it, not because you want to change it.

This seemingly subtle difference changes everything.

Now, don't misunderstand: HAES isn't saying that every single person is healthy at every single weight ever. Instead, "What [HAES] does do is ask for respect and help people shift their focus away from changing their size to enhancing self-care behaviors—so they let weight fall where it may naturally." That's from *Body Respect: What Conventional Health Books Get Wrong, Leave Out, and Just Plain Fail to Understand About Weight*, by Linda Bacon and Lucy Aphramor.[12]

See the difference? Exercising, eating "well," and treating your body like the awesome machine that it is *aren't* evil. Believing that you're a shitty person for not doing those things or that you have to be a certain size to be okay *is*. Again, I encourage you to pick up *Health at Every Size* (or *Body Respect* if you want more of a narrative), because it's seriously worth the read. But for now, I'll give you the CliffsNotes version of three principles the book focuses on.

HAES encourages:

1. Respect, Including Respect for Body Diversity

Yes.

Remember that statistic in the beginning, that only five percent of women naturally possess the body type often portrayed by Americans in the media? Ninety-five percent of us are never gonna have that body naturally. Ever.

But that is NOT what we're told. We're told that we *can* have it, but only if we try hard enough. You say you've tried but still don't look like a photoshopped Megan Fox? Then you're not trying hard *enough*. TRY HARDER.

Isabel Foxen Duke, the creator of the website *Stop Fighting Food* (www.stopfightingfood.com), shared this thought with me so eloquently:

*The myth that our weight is in our exclusive control is more
damaging to women than almost any other social fallacy.
Despite the fact that every conventional beauty standard
that exists is defined fundamentally by its rarity and level of
difficulty to achieve, the myth that humans are in control of
their own body size propels women into the belief that their
inability to attain such standards is their own fault, rather
than the fault of the institutions that create them.*

Bodies come in all shapes and sizes, and the situations they're
born into also affect their shapes and sizes. Bodies are NOT one-size-
fits-all, and it's time we accept and maybe even *embrace* that!

If you want to start working toward that, I'd start implementing
the tips in Chapters 6 and 7, STAT.

2. Compassionate Self-Care

**A. Eating in a flexible and attuned manner that values pleasure
and honors internal cues of hunger, satiety, and appetite.**

I love this principle, because it stops time: It runs in, cuts around all
the bullshit our society has padded around food and its implications,
removes that bullshit, and then runs off . . . leaving us with something
so basic we're surprised we forgot about it at all.

Flexible eating (not to be confused with flexible dieting) is a
fascinating concept: It emphasizes being conscious while consuming
food, enjoying food, staying connected to yourself while eating, and
listening to your body to determine what it needs and when it needs it.
Flexible eating is the opposite of a strict and regimented diet—it allows
us to both reconnect with our bodies and enjoy food. Y'know, minus
the emotional shame/pride/bullshit our society teaches us to associate
with what we consume. We often forget that flexible eating is an option,
because for decades there have been billions of dollars spent to help us
forget about it. But by now you already know that.

So yes, I love this guideline. It goes along with a conversation I had with Isabel Foxen Duke about how we attach SO much to food, and what if, instead of calling it emotional eating, or binge eating, or whatever eating . . . we just called it eating?

Huh. Eating. No guilt. No shame. No pride. No gloating. Just enjoyable consumption of fuel for this body we have that is kinda fucking rad. Yeah. I like it. A LOT.

But of course, with every new solution (however wonderful it is) there are always those who don't have the means to apply it. The go-to advice within body positive groups is sometimes, "If you want Chinese food, order Chinese food, and if you want salad, eat salad!" and there is SO MUCH truth to the idea that giving your body what it wants is important. But what if your body wants something you can't afford? It's a whole other ballgame when you can't change the food that you do or do not have.

As a social worker and someone who grew up poor, I know the solution to poverty is complicated and something that we've been working on, and will need to continue to work on for a long, long, *long* time. But we have to acknowledge that many factors tie into body size and bodies are significantly impacted when there just isn't enough, when living conditions and storage techniques affect what can be kept and what can't, when government food programs give only so many options, when people are forced to choose foods that will last longest, when people have no access to good health care or *any* health care at all, and when people live in "food deserts"—areas where fruits, vegetables, and whole foods just *aren't* available. Anywhere. These are just a few of the factors that affect many people, their bodies, and their self-esteem.

It's fucked up. And messy. And covered with so many other layers of difficulty; meanwhile, society continues to pile more hardships onto people who find themselves in this situation by placing additional layers of guilt and shame around body image and health on top of everything else.

I *don't* have the quick-fix solution for this situation (and another day I want to tell you about how EXACTLY NOT EQUAL opportunity really is for all people), but for now, I just want to bring attention to the fact that this exists, it doesn't need to exist, and adding body image issues on top of other inequalities is not only tragic but unnecessary. Let's work on all of this.

B. Finding the Joy in Moving One's Body and Being Physically Active
We often think that quality exercise in our society happens at a gym, but for me, this has always been a traumatizing experience. Zero joy. Every time I've gone to the gym in my lifetime (there were points when I was there every single day), it has been a form of punishment: a place I needed to go because the current me wasn't good enough, and I needed to run on that treadmill UNTIL I BECAME OKAY, DAMMIT! The gym became a torture chamber, no matter which one I tried (dozens), so gym-related exercise will most likely NOT be pleasurable for me.

But one day I transcended my sordid/ugly/angry/punishing relationship with exercise; it was the day, a couple of years ago, that I had a meltdown. A legit, sobbing, unable-to-fully-understand-what-was-going-on, shaky-body kind of meltdown . . . and it was all over a dance class.

A friend had invited me to Jade Beall's African dance class, and I agreed to go with her; no problemo! But an hour before, my system suddenly realized that I had just signed up for a very new-to-me and very public exercise class, and I went into total shock. Guys, I freaked the fuck out. I felt like I had a momentary break and lost control; it was so unexpected, and at the moment I couldn't even have told you why. I panic-attacked all over my friend's Facebook message box, and our messages back and forth went something like this:

Me, typing, at home in tears:
Nope. I'm not going.
Goddamnit dude, I'm too fucking scared to go.
This body stuff is so HARD.

Nskjdgfsbhkassdfjwsbvgfudjsc.
And I feel totally guilty.
I'm the worst fat person ever.
I'm having a panic attack.
Like crying and shit.
ALL OF THE CRISES.

Friend:
Okay, so what's going on here? What are you really
struggling with?

Me:
Lots of things.
I haven't been in a dance class since college and I'm positive it
will be harder than then and I'm already a physical failure
and I'm positive I'll fail in this class and I don't love my body
today
and I feel like I'm supposed to go and my brain keeps telling
me I have to or else I'm the worst fatty ever
and when I see you I'm just going to regret not going
and then I'll have to sit on my fat ass all night knowing I didn't
do it
when I should have but I can't.
I just can't.

Friend:
Here's the thing.
You're not gonna be the only one. Last time I was there, the
people were all different. There were kids and even an older
man who couldn't move as quickly as everyone else.
It was challenging for everyone.
You're totally not gonna be alone.
And it was challenging for me too! At a certain point I had

to decide that I was either gonna stick through it or get the
fuck out. But I decided to stay and it was amazing and after I
finished I totally felt like I had a dozen orgasms.

Me:
I hate being fat.
I hate everything about it.
I hate how hard it makes daily living
and how many mental barriers I have to fight through just to
do what others do.
And I hate having to justify everything to myself because I feel
like I owe the world to lose weight
or at least try and lose weight or eat differently and lose weight
. . . or something.
It's just really hard and sounds crazy but it's so common for me.
THIS IS ALL OF THE HARDS.

Friend:
I get it.
I totally get it.
Body issues are all of the shit and IT IS ALL OF THE HARDS.
But do yourself a favor, okay? Don't do it for the weight loss.
Just **go for the orgasms.**

So, "for the orgasms" I went. The night turned into a spiritual experience, one that really altered my perspective. Jade is incredible in person. Her infectious energy reminded me that it's important to love others, and even more important, to love yourself. And you should see her shake that incredible booty on the dance floor. God. Damn. And I would estimate that I doubled my friend's record of twelve orgasms in a night. It was. Amazing.

I had to force myself to put on my dance pants *while* I was talking to my friend so I wouldn't back out at the last second. I then turned my brain off and focused solely on my promise to just show up for the warm-up, but I of course stayed for the entire thing. I allowed myself to make mistakes, friends, and a fool out of myself. I wasn't worried about the steps, for the most part, because I had triumphed over my biggest insecurity just by being there.

Now, today, I think back on those Facebook messages without any trace of that emotion. It's hard for me to understand how something as simple as going to a movement class could shake my world so much that I would lose my ability to function. But it did. And it was real. And that sort of freakout is so common.

So often, we fat ladies feel the social pressure to "better ourselves" by losing weight, but then feel ostracized in a workout setting. We feel obligated to join The Perfect Body Factory (okay, maybe you call it a gym), but once there, we feel out of place and pushed into a competition we've failed at before even setting foot inside. It's a mindfuck, and scares a lot of us shitless. The act of combining a fat body and exercise can resurrect a lifetime of shame. One of the most powerful kinds of shame in the world.

I was convinced I would fail that night. I would have bet everything I had in my bank account on it. But I DIDN'T FAIL! I finished the entire class and loved every single minute of it. There was one arm move that confused the shit out of me that I couldn't get down, but that wasn't because of my weight. It was because my brain was like, "WHATTHEFUCK, COUNTING ON OFF-BEATS IS HARD." Sweat was never so rewarding, and I had a lot of it. Well, we all did. I am lucky to be able to see my "before" and "after" emotions and realize that none of this is about obligation, weight loss, or skill sets.

It's about feeling good.

And feeling good is *not* exclusive. Endorphins are not just for those who have perfectly toned bodies. I am allowed to move my body in any way I like and not apologize for the way it looks while doing so. I don't have to be perfect, and I don't have to go for the purpose of changing my body. I can go because I want to. Because I like

THE
**FAT
PEOPLE:**
do all the things!
CHALLENGE
✳

#4: SIT IN A BOOTH.

I surmise that some think fat people shouldn't sit in booths because they would get stuck. And then someone would have to send the waiter into the kitchen to grab the container of clarified butter. And then all the staff would have to cover said fat person with clarified butter and pull on all limbs to get the person free in a coordinated fashion. Fat person would then be asked to not return.

I have NEVER seen that happen. Ever.

So what's the big stink about, then? Booths are my *favorite*! In fact, I ask specifically for them on a regular basis. And I have yet to get mildly stuck. And even if I did, I'm not sure why anyone else would care.

Your challenge: Find a booth and sit in it without apology. Almost anyone can participate. Now, of course, some booths are bigger than others, and some may not be all that comfortable, but if a booth is too small, make it your goal to find one that fits you! There are all kinds of restaurants with booths, lots of them are adjustable, and it kinda sounds like a fun challenge to visit as many restaurants as you want until you find the one that suits you. SO DO IT.

to work the machine I live in. Because I want to feel amazing. Because I deserve to feel amazing.

My advice to every woman who wants to participate in a cycling, aerobics, yoga, Jazzercise, Pilates, swimming, dance, or Zumba class but is scared to try?

Don't go for the weight loss.

Go for the orgasms.

Another way to approach physical movement for fat bodies is with the idea that maybe we fatties need it even more than others. No, NOT because we need to become un-fat, or because we should exercise more than others as a form of repentance, but rather because of self-hatred, which can distance us from our bodies. When body hatred abounds, our relationship with our outside suffers. As Hanne Blank, in her amazing book, *The Unapologetic Fat Girl's Guide to Exercise and Other Incendiary Acts*, says, movement can be used as the tool that helps us connect with all of us again. Movement can rebuild our relationship with our wonderful fat bodies. I absolutely love this concept. We deserve to feel whole, connected, and at home within our skin as well.

When it comes to exercise and fitness, I want to make sure that I'm clear: There are some people out there who have found immense joy in these two things. It's their hobby, their love, and the center of their life. This is *good*. It makes them happy, and I'm happy that they're happy. YOU SHOULD ALWAYS DO WHAT MAKES YOU HAPPY! But you do not need to make fitness and exercise the focal point of your life if you don't want to. It doesn't make you a failure. It doesn't make you a bad person. It doesn't decrease your worth. It makes you a person who is awesome enough to choose what's important to you.

At the time of print, the HAES website was being updated to include a final concept:

3. Critical Awareness

A. challenges scientific and cultural assumptions and B. values body knowledge and people's lived experiences. I love the addition of these key ideas and can vouch for their importance as we covered both in this book previously. In order to fully connect with our bodies and treat them with compassion we *must* allow ourselves to question the status quo (however counterintuitive that may seem) and acknowledge that we are unique beings with personal histories and understandings that influence the way we exist within this world. FUCK YEAH, HAES!

"Okay, but Jeeeeees, you're avoiding the question everyone asks! Aren't there fat people who don't have a 'clean bill of health'?" SURE! There are fat bodies with high blood pressure and cholesterol and diabetes (there are thin bodies who have all of those things too, but the world forgets that part). This is going to be shocking to some, but here's what I think about "unhealthy" bodies (of all shapes and sizes): They are just as wonderful, perfect and deserving of self-love as all other bodies.

You heard me.

We all deserve the same amount of opportunity, respect, health care, education, life, love, liberty, and the pursuit of happiness regardless of our size, shade, shape, sex, gender, level of ability, and health records.

You can quote me on that.

So my point? Regardless of your health and body size, know that you are worthy of body love.

Yes, people love to ask if I'm glorifying obesity by promoting body love.

To that I say: It's so so SO much bigger than that question, but if you're *really* concerned about *health*, you'll ignore the largely irrelevant factor of weight and focus on more significant issues like making sure people can afford nutritious food and have access to education that allows them to provide for their families. You might also focus on providing unbiased health care, and helping to destigmatize mental illness so people can find resources and feel supported, which then allows for physically healthy lives. (Surprise! Mean people generally don't like that answer.)

But REGARDLESS (yes, regardless) of health: I believe in glorifying *all bodies*. All of them. Because every single person in the entire world deserves to feel good about and love themselves. It's that simple. Fat and thin, healthy and unhealthy.

So y'know what else I glorify?

I glorify HAPPINESS.

Simply put: **glorifying happiness = being invested in the belief that everyone deserves to love their bodies.**

It seems like such an elementary concept, yet somehow it's one of the world's most controversial. So what about you? Do you believe that everyone deserves a chance to love their bodies? Do you believe that everyone deserves a chance to be happy no matter their size or shape?

You do?!?!? Well, I do, too. WE SHOULD PROBABLY BECOME FRIENDS.

And after we become friends, I'm going to point out that *I just tricked you into saying that YOU deserve to love YOUR body no matter what it looks like.* ZING. I gotcha. You're part of everyone, my love, and if I deserve to love my body, and she deserves to love her body, and he deserves to love his body, and they deserve to love their body . . . then that means you deserve to love your body, too. No matter your shape, size, shade, sex, or age, YOU deserve to be glorified. You deserve that happiness, too.

GOOD HEALTH CARE
COMES WITH SELF-ADVOCACY
JEN MCLELLAN OF PLUS SIZE BIRTH

H ealth care may not be the sexiest topic, but it sure is an important one.

Oftentimes care providers come with their own biases, but you might forget this . . . that is, until you're sitting half-dressed in your doctor's office being shamed because of your weight.

Studies show that when patients are shamed by their health care provider they are less likely to get routine medical care and more likely to gain weight.[1] It's time we stop hoping our care providers will treat us with dignity and start expecting it! After all, these people work for us, and we pay them our hard-earned money for their medical expertise.

One of the best ways to advocate for your health care is to hire a size-friendly provider. This is a medical professional who practices evidence-based, compassionate care. He or she is a provider who doesn't just equate good health with a low number on the Body Mass Index (BMI) chart.

How do you find a size-friendly health care provider? The best place to start is by reaching out to your friends of all sizes, but especially your fat friends. Do they have a doctor they like? If the answer is yes, write down that provider's contact information. You can also ask your coworkers, because they usually have the same insurance provider you do. Aside from talking to people you know, there are a few websites that have lists of size-friendly providers, including haescommunity.org, plussizebirth.com, and fatfriendlydocs.com

The midwifery model of health care is often overlooked because people assume midwives only work with pregnant women, but this isn't the case! Midwives often practice woman-centered care and look at your whole health history, not just a particular diagnosis you've received. They also tend to be more size friendly, so consider hiring a midwife for your well-woman appointments.

Once you have a few referrals it's time to Google any prospective care providers. Yes, just like you'd scope out a potential date! Do a little research to see if any red flags pop up, like horrendous reviews. On the flip side, you might find a lot of positive information that could actually make you excited to set up a doctor's appointment.

Use the initial Google investigation to narrow down your list. Next, call care providers' offices and speak to the front office staff— the gatekeepers. You'll want to ask some questions to pare down your list even further. Does their office see people of all sizes? Do they have larger gowns? What about different-sized blood pressure cuffs? If they don't have large blood pressure cuffs, that should be a deal breaker. An inaccurate reading can label you as having high blood pressure and lead to an unnecessary and potentially harmful prescription. This happens more often than you'd believe.

It's unlikely you can get a phone or in-person interview with the care provider you are considering, but it doesn't hurt to ask. What you can do is drop by your selected doctor's office in person. That way you can make some observations and perhaps get a few minutes of their time.

Speaking of observations, that's your next task. Once you arrive at your new or current doctor's office, you'll want to take note of the waiting room. Do all of the chairs have arms or is there a place for you to sit comfortably? Review the brochures in the waiting room, posters, and other promotional materials. How body positive is the environment?

Once you're called back to see the nurse, it's time to start advocating for yourself. Make sure they use that large blood pressure cuff if you need it. If you would prefer not to be weighed you will most likely be met with pushback, but stick up for yourself. You have the right to refuse any medical test you're uncomfortable with. Though if you're working with a size-friendly provider, weight is just one of many measurements they will look at. Speaking of weight, what does the scale go up to?

Going to the doctor can make some people incredibly anxious (talk about cause for a high blood-pressure reading). If you're one of those people, you don't need to do this alone. Bring along a partner, family member, or close friend.

Now it's time to see your care provider, ask questions, and make more observations. When it feels like the right time to ask questions, take a deep breath and try to relax the best you can (here's where some eye contact with a support person can be really beneficial). You want to open up an honest line of communication, so make an effort not to come across as defensive. Writing down your questions in advance can be really helpful.

Ask anything that's important to you. There are no silly questions when it comes to your health care! Here are a few suggestions: How importantly do you view weight? I'm concerned you may focus on my weight instead of my overall health. What other ways, aside from weight, can we measure improvement (for example, blood pressure, blood sugar, cholesterol, and other tests)? Do you know about Health at Every Size (HAES)? If not, I'd like to talk with you about it.

While you're asking questions do some more observations. Is your care provider watching the clock and making you feel rushed, or is he or she listening to and addressing your concerns? Did the provider relate all of your medical concerns to your weight, or look at the big picture of your overall health? Talking about diet and exercise isn't inherently stigmatizing, but you'll want to listen to the way they discuss them. Remember, it is okay to disagree with your doctor as long as you're both part of a team and can be honest with each other.

Finally, you'll want to trust your gut when deciding if your care provider is size friendly or not. After you leave the provider's office, how do you feel? Look over the answers to all of the questions you asked and review the observations you made. You should know fairly quickly whether this provider is a good fit for you. Please note that you have the right to refuse any medical intervention, get a second opinion, or fire your care provider at any time. You owe it to yourself to prioritize your health and connect with a care provider who treats you with compassion.

✳

selfies aren't selfish: narcissism is good for you

[CHAPTER SIX]

You heard me right. Selfies are not only *not* selfish, they're absolutely necessary. It's the truth, and I'm sticking by it.

At every lecture, I ask the audience who *hasn't* heard of Photoshop. I have yet to see someone raise their hand. We all know what it is, that it's prevalent (it's now a verb in the dictionary), and that the way it's used to "perfect" and alter bodies in photos is more or less (okay, it's more) bullshit. BUT STILL, our brain, as it walks by the magazines at the grocery store on the way to check out, doesn't always register this concept. Our conscious critique of realistic images isn't running at full speed, but the pictures and ads we see in passing do in fact affect us. Even if we don't know it.

Do me a favor. Google "celebrity photoshop."

Did you find hundreds of images that show how distorted our concept of acceptable and realistic beauty truly is? Yeah, it's everywhere. If you didn't Google that just now, I'll go ahead and share what you'll find: a "before" picture of Beyoncé, and an "after" one where her waist has been cinched, legs slimmed, and skin lightened. You'll find Madonna's "before" and then "after" with all her age lines removed, skin brightened, and cleavage increased. You can even find George Clooney (whom some consider the most handsome older gent in the land) with an "after" picture of him sans wrinkles, and with a thinner face. Even celebrity "street style" and performance photos are altered. Yet how often while in line at the grocery store do we take the time to think, *god, those cover models don't look anything like that in real life*, and if we do, do we understand the depth and breadth of the alterations? How often do we just subconsciously categorize the images as normal and representative of real life, when in actuality they don't exist anywhere? I think we all have some awareness of the visual lie, but I don't think we realize the extent and how much it affects our psyche. The cover models not only don't exist now; they never will.

I've watched countless smart and brilliant women buy into the digitally altered version of people and make matching that look their most important goal. The "inspiration" surrounding us goes far beyond ridiculous and unattainable. Tina Fey captures the absurdity of it:

Now every girl is expected to have:

- *Caucasian blue eyes*
- *full Spanish lips*
- *a classic button nose*
- *hairless Asian skin with a California tan*
- *a Jamaican dance hall ass*
- *long Swedish legs*
- *small Japanese feet*
- *the abs of a lesbian gym owner*
- *the hips of a nine-year-old boy*

- *the arms of Michelle Obama*
- *and doll tits.*

The person closest to actually achieving this look is Kim Kardashian, who, as we know, was made by Russian scientists to sabotage our athletes.[1]

This is why we are all struggling.

And just so you know, Kim Kardashian has cellulite, and though I haven't chatted with her lately, I'm sure she has her own insecurities just like everyone else. Because NO ONE is "perfect" in the eyes of society's standards. Not even her.

But fortunately, we have options. In order to address this outrageous issue, we can and must: **(1) Consciously (and repeatedly) acknowledge that photo editing software is heavily relied upon to alter the images we see in media** and **(2) counter the prevalence of digital alteration by taking authentic (read: unaltered) images of ourselves**. I'm totally talking about selfies, y'all.

Because the average American sees nearly three thousand advertisements and hundreds of images a day (that more than likely don't include what they see in the mirror), WE MUST counter this with our own alternatives; we must balance out the bullshit with reality.[2] We must create a safe space for ourselves and our bodies to exist.

Selfies and self-portraits have been a powerful tool for me since the beginning of my fat acceptance days. When I first started blogging about body image, I joined in on a challenge put forth by Rachele of *The Nearsighted Owl* called "I Am Proud of My Size." The goal was for bloggers to take full-body pictures of themselves and post them unapologetically . . . with their sizes listed. At the time, this was the ultimate step outside my comfort zone.

Always enthralled with a challenge, I posted images weekly, bolstered by the support of other bloggers who participated. As time progressed, I started to learn a lot about my relationship with my body.

How it really looked to the world, how that felt, and the fact that I only felt comfortable presenting it in poses that I deemed "flattering." It was a pretty limited repertoire, and mostly consisted of a hand on my hip with my stomach sucked in and my double chin hidden. Some called it a "teacup"; I called it flattering.

In the beginning, it felt reckless to post even these posed images . . . I was daring to document ALL of me, and that was radical. But as I shared these images more and more, I noticed that no one was blinded, traumatized, or offended. No one died. No one stabbed their eyes out, and in fact, I was pleasantly surprised to see that the feedback was occasionally positive and complimentary. It seems obvious, right? But it was new to me after being SO conditioned to hate myself. I honest to god didn't think that would be the outcome.

Emboldened, I wrote a post where I broke up with Flattering. The letter went like this:

> *Dear Flattering,*
> *I'm so over you.*
> *Because of you, I only take certain pictures with certain poses with certain outfits. You're (pretty much) kinda boring. So, it's over. Maybe we can get together again in the future . . .*
> *if you're lucky.*
> *Till then,*
> *Jes*

I then proceeded to take jumping pictures (because apparently that's what we bloggers do), the likes of which include some of the most "unflattering" faces I've ever made. It was motherfucking liberating, guys. And ever since then, I've continued to widen my pose options, much to my personal delight.

The *Oxford Dictionary* defines "selfie" as "a photograph that one has taken of oneself, typically one taken with a smartphone or webcam and shared via social media."[3]

When I read this, I was highly entertained by the sample sentence that followed: "Occasional selfies are acceptable, but posting a new picture of yourself everyday isn't necessary." This villainizing of self-portraits, my friends, is EXACTLY why taking selfies is so important.

I had the enormous pleasure of talking with Vivienne McMasters, who in real life is the Selfie Championess. She owns and runs "Be Your Own Beloved," an empowerment technique and curriculum in which you learn to "[cultivate] self-love through self-portraiture." In other words, you learn to love yourself through selfies.

During our chat (when I wasn't distracted by her amazing Vancouver accent), we talked about her mission to bring women closer to themselves through the act of capturing themselves on camera. She mentioned that one of the first questions she's asked when teaching selfie workshops is, "How are they NOT selfish?" It seems so vain to us, right? We're shamed into thinking that any exploration of our physical self is narcissistic and egocentric.

Oh, this is not the case at all.

Vivienne explained that she started taking self-portraits as a way of giving herself space and to reconnect with herself. What ended up happening was that the second she set the camera timer, the negative body voices were quieted, and she felt like for the first time she got to define how she saw herself. To her, it felt beautiful.

> *It's hard to explain to others, and hard for them to believe that if they try taking photos of themselves—which is totally scary for a lot of people—that they might find that feeling of self-empowerment because they get to define how they see themselves. You can definitely find proof that your body is beautiful and fabulous and that it's more incredible than you ever thought you could see in a photo. You'll have the chance to see yourself in a really authentic way reflected. I feel like it not only helps people visually see themselves in a different light, but it also helps reconnect us. And that is certainly not selfish.*

Taking selfies, Vivienne explained, gives us the opportunity to create our own narratives, to tell our own stories. In her lectures, she talks about articles she often sees online saying selfies are "dangerous," and that taking and posting selfies is an addiction. One article describes how to stop taking self-portraits, comparing it to weaning yourself off other harmful addictions like cocaine or alcohol.

I suppose there could be a bit of danger in taking unaltered selfies: the danger that it challenges everything you've ever been taught, like: *Loathe your body. Take up as little space as possible. Be self-effacing and humble.* A perfect combination of sexism and body hate is the real reason selfies are mocked by those who have their own insecurities and who give zero shits about us and a million shits about a market growing richer by the day by promoting self–loathing. I'm only gonna say this once: Fuck the system; take some selfies.

Okay, fine, I'll say it again. **Fuck the system; take some selfies.**

I feel like that would make a great hashtag.

The list of "Things That Exist Everywhere in the Real World but Are Airbrushed Out of Every Magazine Spread" is a mile long, but I'll start with this short list of **five things that are often photoshopped out that I want to see more of: cellulite, diversity of races and shades, post-birth bodies, wrinkle lines, and non-hourglass plus-sized women.**

It sounds like I'm shooting for the moon, right? That's because I am.

Cellulite. Almost all women have it (close to 90 percent, in fact), but guess what? As normal as it is, in 2012 alone we spent nearly $8 million on clinical cellulite treatment.[4] The home-based anti-cellulite industry rakes in another estimated $62 million after convincing us that our "orange-peel," "cottage-cheese," and "hail-damaged" skin is not only a visual abomination but proof of our lack of self-control.

If only we exercised more and ate better!

Nope. Not it.

Although it's treated as a flaw, cellulite is simply a fat storage situation. The Mayo Clinic explains: "Cellulite is caused by fibrous connective cords that tether the skin to the underlying muscle, with the fat lying between. As fat cells accumulate, they push up against the skin, while the long, tough cords pull down. This creates an uneven surface or dimpling."[5]

In short, fat women have cellulite, skinny women have cellulite, famous people have cellulite, ballerinas have cellulite, personal trainers have cellulite, models have cellulite, runners have cellulite, women who still live in indigenous, hunter-gatherer communities have cellulite, and women who have had plastic surgery (there's no "permanent cure") have cellulite. If you were to fill a room with women of all shapes and sizes, most of those women would have cellulite. Because it's totally and completely normal.

> **There is nothing wrong with your body if you've got some dimples. Or a million dimples. Or if your dimples have dimples.**

Why don't men have as much cellulite? Well, (1) their skin is thicker so it shows less, and (2) they store more fat around their organs instead of between the skin and muscle like we do.

Structural. Mechanics. Period.

My point? There is nothing wrong with your body if you've got some dimples. Or a million dimples. Or if your dimples have dimples. There's no "cure," and no need for one. It's not a measuring device for your self-worth. And you're not the only one who has it, no matter what those glossy spreads say.

Diversity of races and shades. The "white ideal," much like the thin ideal, is created to exclude certain racial identities, to encourage self-hate and then create a market selling the antidote to that created self-hate. The white ideal and the perpetuation of the white ideal purposefully excludes women of color from our (very limited) definition of beauty. Much like the way bodies are "thinned out" in images, skin tones are lightened to systemically absorb bodies into the concept that "lighter is better."

The act itself is called "whitewashing," and it is just one more way havoc is wreaked upon bodies by underrepresentation and exclusion of those outside of the carefully crafted "norm."

Pia Schiavo-Campo of the blog *Chronicles of a Mixed Fat Chick* lectures about this very concept:

> *Whitewashing strips away all the beauty and nuanced differences that make up our diverse world. When light-skinned ethnic models with Caucasian features are used in advertisements that are meant to be "inclusive," we are telling women that it's ok to be different, just not too different—not too far from white. It leaves little room for seeing ourselves represented in the media. This kind of propaganda is one of the many ways in which racism is perpetuated in subtle ways.[6]*

We see so much diversity erasure arising from this elimination of skin shades here in the U.S., and it is so significant that it transfers across the globe. There is a dangerous (like, kidney-failure danger-ous) trend in Nigeria, where 80 percent of women regularly use skin lighteners. But, as one woman shared online, "I'm not seeking to be totally white, I just want to be beautiful."

Fuck.

We as a culture are just now starting to place a small empha-sis on "diversity," and are occasionally including women of color in the media. But if you look closely, these popularized faces are often those who have lighter skin, straight or wavy hair, and facial features that are considered more or less "Caucasian." This is far from inclusive and far from diverse. Yet companies with unlim-ited resources pat themselves on the back, saying, "LOOK HOW PROGRESSIVE WE ARE!"

Nope.

This is exactly what Sonya Renee Taylor talks about in her article, "Weighting to Be Seen" (that we read at the end of Chapter 3): Not being invited to the "table," where white women have always been allowed (as long as they fit into the chair).

Now, with the pushing of boundaries, I'd say that progress has been made so that some white women who DON'T fit into the chair are invited to bring their own. It's FUCKED to have to bring your own chair, but you know what's worse? Being invited to bring your own chair but ONLY if you alter your appearance so that when you arrive you no longer look like yourself.

That's not really an invitation, my friends.

That seat doesn't count for shit.

When we refuse to allow all races to have equal visibility, we are not just sending a message to individuals that they are "not worthy of taking up space" but we are also contributing to larger systemic issues like racial discrimination, hatred, and violence. Yes, it is *that* big of a deal.

I'd love to see a wide range of races, shades, and colors in images *all over* the web. This representation will not only be beautiful, but immensely powerful and necessary if we are going to embrace and respect the variety of bodies that we have in real life.

Post-birth bodies. Another idea we see glorified in the media is the ridiculous assumption that any woman worth her salt should have a body that "bounces back" after childbirth. I've never had a child, but I've watched my friends and others struggle with adjusting to post-birth bodies and the lasting changes that come with childbearing. The stripes. The loss of elasticity. The pouch or "mothers apron" as I learned it is sometimes called. The deflation of the boobs. The scars. All of these things affected my friends' self-esteem in some way—it was agonizing for me just to watch how they struggled, so I can't even imagine how difficult it must be for them to experience. I once asked my followers on Facebook this question: "Mothers: What was the hardest part of your body to love after having a child?" In less than an hour, there were over six hundred comments listing everything mentioned above. The struggle to love a changing body is so pertinent, and no one is alone in this.

#5: MAKE YOUR BODY YOUR ART.

Making art based on your body can be an amazingly transformative experience. For me, painting pictures of my body stops me enough to . . . look. To see the details of my body. I can't judge it when I'm up close and concentrating on brushstrokes. Working the paint to recreate my folds. Taking the time to shade my belly button. To see how the shadows fall and rise with the rolling stomach I own. It really puts a new perspective on something I see every day. When I stood back to view my first painting of my torso, I thought, "That's kind of a great painting!" And THEN I thought, "Ohmygod, that's my body. And I liked it before I realized it . . . so I must like my body after all!"

Your challenge: Create art featuring YOU! Use any medium you like: paint, computer, collage, photography, sculpture . . . anything. Make something frame-worthy—after all, your body already is.

Because this is a significant issue, I consulted a professional—by "professional," I mean a good friend who also lives here in Tucson, who's kind of a big deal in the Mom World. Jade, of Jade Beall Photography, has made an international name for herself by specializing in what she calls "medicinal photography for mothers." Essentially, she's all about creating un-photoshopped and intimate images of women and their bodies (and children) after giving birth. She has assisted in creating a subculture where all of these stripes, scars, and pouches are viewed as beautiful. It's kind of magical.

In contrast, there are altered images of new moms all over our tabloid magazines with praises sung to those who show no signs of creating life. We talk about their "stunning post-baby body evolution," and we compliment those who look like they never had another human inside them. I'll never forget seeing a magazine cover that showed Kate Middleton tossing a basketball, with accompanying commentary about how sexy her flawless post-pregnancy body was. She was also missing a belly button. Total photoshop fail. Way to make even more women insecure about their own bodies, guys.

> **Another idea we see glorified in the media is the ridiculous assumption that any woman worth her salt should have a body that "bounces back" after childbirth.**

Don't misunderstand: There will definitely be those with bodies that are predispositioned to return to their former shape sans stretch marks and other changes, and this is totally okay and wonderful! But those are few and far between. Jade is all about helping *all* mamas fall in love with their "new bodies," just the way they are.

Over coffee, Jade pointed out that most of the "bounce-back" bodies we see online *have* been altered. "Maria Kang," she said, "the 'Fit Mom,' is a perfect example. She *has* stretch marks, but in the beginning they weren't visible in her images." (Note: I didn't believe Jade, so I researched it, and sure as shit . . .) But when Maria started getting push back, she started posting photos *with* the stretch marks—with her real skin. Proof that even these "celebrated bodies" have marks and all of the things we don't like about ourselves. "When we look at mothers' bodies in the media, we're not looking at them," Jade said, "we're looking at an unrealistic rendition of them."

Her advice for moms struggling to accept their post-birth bodies fell right in line with the premise of this chapter: Start by taking lots of selfies. Look at them and try to find the beauty, even if you need to "fake it until you make it." Find images of bodies online that look like yours. "Social media is such a rad tool," Jade told me. "We get to follow people who empower us. There is something powerful about being seen. So find a community that can see YOU for the beautiful person that you are!"

Wrinkles. We have literally tried to erase wrinkles from our world through softening, digital cloning tools, and beauty products alike.

But guess what's never actually disappeared from real life, no matter how much we try? Wrinkles. As Jade said to me, "We're erasing signs of having lived. These things just . . . say that we've had a massive experience called life!"

Our race toward thin often overlaps with our need for youth, and because of this, older bodies are purposefully hidden away while younger ones take their place. We try to escape the inevitable—outrun death—and in doing so we play right into the advertisers' dreams. I can hear them now: *What can't be stopped by anyone in the entire world even with all of our brilliant technology? I know! GETTING OLDER! Let's tell them that they need to always stay young in order to be okay!*

As Naomi Wolf notes, when there is speculation that Elizabeth Hurley was fired as Estee Lauder's spokesperson because supposedly "the world" believed that her thirty-six-year-old body was *too* old . . . well, you do have to wonder how fucked our standard for aging really is.[7]

The issue with this is not only does it fuck with the minds of those grappling with aging, but it also diminishes the importance of those who have aged already. Where are our older women? Over 108 billion people have lived and aged on this earth, and every single person alive eventually fits into this category, yet we don't seem to see any of them represented in the media.[8] I used to think that the reason we didn't see older bodies was because they had already caught on to the bullshit we younger generations believe and had transcended body image issues. But I was wrong.

Here's the thing. A large percentage of older women are not only dissatisfied with their size (same as most of us), but they are also not okay with other effects of aging. They're having a hard time in general, goddamnit. And the women who ARE okay with their size (a measly 12 percent) still have aging to deal with.[9] Things don't get better in the body image world as we get older.

So here's what we need to do: We need to give visibility to older bodies. Period. We need to remove them from the shadows and give them a voice in this world where they are also struggling with being erased. Me, I want more wrinkles, damn it. More of every sign of aging. Weight is not a determinant of beauty, and neither is age.

Non-hourglass fat people. I'm not sure if you've noticed (I'm pretty sure you've noticed), but ever since we as a culture have started to include plus models in our fashion spreads and pictures, they've only come in one shape: the sort of shape that has a waistline *considerably* smaller than the bust and hips. It's everywhere, and it's the *only representation* of a larger body that is deemed acceptable in our mainstream advertising. It's SO important, apparently, that models with not "enough" of an hourglass figure are padded underneath their clothes and then waists are nipped and tucked, rolls are eliminated, and all kinds of other digital voodoo happens to make sure we never see any other version than the "coke bottle figure." ANY perpetuation of one universal body standard ain't good for us, this one included.

BUT, in the same breath, I'm also gonna acknowledge that including the hourglass figure in the media is much-needed progress. There was a time when showing *any* larger shape was unheard of. But I think it's time to be realistic about how *unrealistic* and fabricated this hourglass standard is and think about what it will take to normalize all fat body shapes.

I love what Charing Ball has to say in her article on *Madame Noire*, "More Than the Coke Bottle Look: Why Plus Size Isn't as Diverse as It Should Be":

> *The term "plus size" [in fashion] doesn't seek to counteract the idealized waif image by showing beauty in all shapes and sizes, but rather, reinforces the notion that beauty has its limits.*
> *And more often than not, it tends to create new ways in which women and girls can learn to feel bad about themselves. While*

seeing bigger women is an improvement and empowering in itself, if all we are really seeing is bigger versions of the same image we've been force-fed since we were kids, all we are really doing is trading in one oppression for another.[10]

A perfect example of this: In 2010, *V* Magazine published a spread called "One Size Fits ALL" showing two models—one straight-sized and one plus-sized—dressed in the exact same outfit. But the two models' hourglass proportions are identical: If you didn't give it a long hard look, you might think the magazine simply enlarged the first model's photo to take up more space. So while we're starting to see value in unconventional bodies, there is still one "right" way for those bodies to look. Our "junk" must appropriately bookend our midsections, or else it's wrong. More progress, plz.

When I participated in a consumer study for a fashion company recently, I and the other plus women—all advocates for inclusive body acceptance—at the table were handed "flash cards," each of which featured an image of a large-bodied woman, and were asked to sort them in order of consumer acceptability. It turned out that, as a group, we rated as the most "acceptable" those women's bodies who were merely larger versions of the bodies of traditional models. The least "acceptable" types leaned toward the square- and apple-shaped silhouettes. Our ratings had nothing to do with style, hair color, tattoos, or confidence, but rather how much each body fit the ideal of the "perfect hourglass woman." It just goes to show that even those of us who are working to change things have been trained to think this way.

It's unfortunate, not only because of the general perpetuation of unfair standards, but also because it creates a form of privilege among those who *do* have this body type. While I personally deal with an extraordinary amount of backlash due to my fat body, I am fully aware that I also receive more positive attention than those who may not have an hourglass figure do. I'm NOT padded and digitally cinched, but because I align (ever so slightly, mind you) with the industry standard,

I can't help but notice that other advocates who *don't* align have a disparaging following that is much, MUCH larger.

I mean, look at the cover of this book, for example. While she's an illustration, she has a hardcore hourglass shape and that image was chosen by the design team because they knew readers would feel more comfortable picking up a book with this type of silhouette on it. And YEAH! It's *really* important for people to pick up the book; I wouldn't have taken the time to write the damn thing if it wasn't! But let's just acknowledge that this is a perfect example of how we are still only comfortable with one version of fat.

> **I hope that soon we will be barraged with not just hourglass-shaped plus bodies, but also square-shaped plus bodies, and apple-shaped plus bodies, pizza-shaped plus bodies, Frisbee-shaped bodies, and Lumpy Space Princess–shaped plus bodies.**

For the record, I think it's amazing that this book, title, and cover has even gone to print. And y'know what? This beautiful woman *does exist* somewhere and I'm honored she's gracing the front of this handbook you're holding. Things like this remind me that we're definitely seeing more body positive exploration in our media nowadays and this is fucking great. YAY WORLD! But the real talk is: The concept of embracing *all* body types (non-hourglass fat ones too!) is still in its infant stages.

It's my hope that our narrow-minded society quickly acclimates to seeing larger bodies, so that we are able to successfully integrate ALL shapes and sizes.

I hope that soon we will be barraged with not just hourglass-shaped plus bodies, but also square-shaped plus bodies, and apple-shaped plus bodies, pizza-shaped plus bodies, Frisbee-shaped bodies, and Lumpy Space Princess–shaped plus bodies and . . . I've forgotten where I was going with this.

I wanna see ALL the kinds of fat bodies represented sooner rather than later, please. Not just nipped, tucked, altered to be more "slender in the middle" fat bodies. THAT's where I was going with that!

Truth time: We don't see enough cellulite, stretch marks, wrinkles, racial diversity, or non-hourglass fat bodies represented . . . well, anywhere. They've been clone stamped, softened, and erased from our images, but there's good news. There's a place where it all stops, and that's with you. And me. And anyone else who's interested in filling the Internet with un-photoshopped images of themselves. If you have any (or all) of those five things (or anything else on the list that goes unrepresented), TAKE A SELFIE and create a space online where your body exists. *We can change the photoshop culture with our phones, y'all.* Just by taking images of real life and sharing them with the world. If you're not feeling publicly brazen yet, you can try taking selfies just for yourself as a way of exploring your own story and relationship with your body.

You *don't* necessarily need to start out by taking pictures of your dimply ass and posting them on Instagram (but if you do, make sure you tag #BootyRevolution so Meghan Tonjes and I can see your contribution to the beautiful online butt collection); you can start out by taking a traditional selfie. This first step could be the catalyst for many more self-portrait revelations in your future.

I've compiled six tips for taking selfies that have nothing to do with making you look "better," but rather serve as starting points that will allow you to take whatever kind of image you desire.

Six Tips for Taking Selfies

1. Start gently. Guyz. You don't need to jump straight into nude, full-body waters. If you're hesitant about capturing yourself in the first place, try using the mirror in a bathroom or somewhere else that feels private and safe.

Take selfies *however you want to take them.* From way up high, or down low . . . there is no wrong way to take a selfie. Whatever it takes to make you feel good! Do your duck lips, do your poses, do whatever makes you feel best.

When photographers take photos of people, they all know that a moving subject can look different in every frame. But that doesn't make one image more "truthful" than others. Take pictures of yourself however you want. They're all you.

After becoming comfortable with this, Vivienne suggests attempting to show your hands or feet in the photo. Sounds too simplistic? Then go for broke and get your whole self in there. It's what works for Vivienne: "The most transformative kind of selfie, the one that feels transformative for me, is one where your entire body is in the photo. Because then we do get to see ourselves as a whole."

My personal experience is that with every full-body shot I capture, I sink a teeny bit further into complete and total body love. It's gradual, but effective.

2. Tell a story. Our photos give us the opportunity to tell the story of us. Photos can be a literal, visual representation of our body, sure, but they are also a way for us to share a little bit about who we are. Think about taking up physical space and how it can reveal something about yourself. Or choose something to wear that says something about you that others may not know. Notice how the moments when you break into laughter can bring intimacy to your photos. There's a lot your photos can say.

You're in charge of the narrative. Write it your way.

3. Ask your body what it wants to do. If you're jonesing for freedom, think outside the box, as I did when I broke up with Flattering. Ask yourself: "What does my body want to do?" Does it want to stand? Does it want to sit? Does it want to lie in the grass? Does it want to jump? Whatever YOUR body wants to do, do THAT.

Many of Vivienne's photos show her dancing. "I always felt like I needed to sit still and be contained," she writes. "To not bother anyone; to sit on my hands and shrink myself down. . . . It's not just about [dancing] . . . it's that I'm taking up space and allowing myself to be expansive and fuck anyone who tells me that I need to pose in a smaller way."

Teacup pose be damned.

Unless you like the teacup pose. Then you should totally rock it.

4. Look for *yourself* in the photos. This is perhaps the most important part. We do this terrible thing where we look in the mirror or at pictures and we expect to see a thin model. Unless you *are* a thin model, THIS WILL NEVER HAPPEN. So stop that shit. The second you start looking for *you* is the second you will start to appreciate what you are. Stop looking for flaws. Stop looking for differences. There is not one definition of beauty. Try to see yourself with kindness. You are absolutely perfect just as you are. Try to find *that*.

5. Show your images to someone else. This is critical as well. We sometimes have the urge to hide hard things from others. We only put our "best" pictures on Facebook, and we "un-tag" images of us that we hate that our friends add. I'm going to ask you to do the opposite of that.

When you look at your images, sit with them for a while (hopefully you'll love them!), and then show them to someone, whether it be your lover, your partner, a friend, your social media network . . . just show someone you trust.

I had a terrifying experience at a nude shoot with a hundred other women where we used our bodies to create image diversity that we could share with the Internet. In a moment of encouragement for others to be brave, I stripped down to nothing and struck a powerful pose. When I saw the image of myself that had been taken . . . well, I kinda lost it. I hated it more than I've ever hated an image of myself before. I felt that I looked "too masculine," and my short hair only seemed to exacerbate this. I saw the "flaws." I saw that belly.

I sat on the image for weeks, loathing my body until I just couldn't take it anymore. I had to know if it was as awful as my critical mind said it was. So with tears in my eyes, I sat down with my boyfriend and showed it to him. Guess what he saw? A goddamn sexy woman he was in love with.

We certainly don't need to define our worth by what others think of us, but we also don't need to ignore the fact that sometimes support is helpful and needed. Our perception of ourselves is often skewed because of our lifetime of shame, and sometimes the outside perspective of someone who "sees us" as we really are is a gift.

So share them! Throw them up on Facebook. Watch people not die. They might even compliment you, and I'm gonna suggest that you don't deflect it. Yeah, that's right. Take the compliments. I'm giving you ALL of the challenges right now, aren't I?

6. HAVE FUN! Have *so* much fun. This is about you, and celebrating you. Despite what you've been told, selfies are not dangerous, vainglorious, or conceited. They are a tool for reclamation. For seeing yourself through your own eyes. For defining what you believe is worthy. So call all the shots, be the boss, do you, and celebrate!

Call out photoshopping for the insidious scoundrel it is, reclaim your body by creating your own narrative through selfies, and then share the shit out of the images and flood the world with unaltered beauty. All un-photoshopped pictures add an element of truth to an otherwise airbrushed world.

THAT is how you fuck the system.

From the inside out.

*

change your tumblr, change your life: diversify your media feed

[CHAPTER SEVEN]

'm most *certainly* not the activist who is going to tell you to turn off your television and burn all of your magazines. As someone who works online all day and loves to critique pop culture, I think that sounds like a life worse than hell. Wait, I'm assuming that Netflix counts as television, right? If so, fuck that shit.

I do have another suggestion though, and it's REALLY simple. Simple as in: Click your mouse a few times and watch your world change.

Intrigued? Thought so. I'll explain.

I have an old guilty pleasure television show called *Pregnant in Heels*. For those of you who haven't seen or heard of this show (you're not really missing anything), it's about a London-born former ballet dancer and model named Rosie Pope. Rosie now dedicates her life to saving wealthy future parents from themselves, and coaches them on everything from choosing a bassinet to improving pregnant sex. It's on Bravo, *obviously*.

So, here's the thing: Despite the fact that it's classist, totally inapplicable to most of the world, and seemingly heavily scripted, there are elements of actual factual life found within. Namely, that Rosie Pope exists in real life. Her svelte figure, thigh gap, and Pantene-sanctioned hair EXISTS. But guess what else is part of actual factual life? That statistic that 95 percent of women do *not* have the body of Rosie Pope (or anyone else we see presented as "attractive" in our media), which is pretty much almost everybody else. Rosie Pope isn't everybody else, and it's easy to forget that.

What should you do to counter media like this? **Diversify your media feed.**

This is where your personal power trumps all. We spend more time on our media feeds than we do our pets.[1] If you allow your media feed to regulate itself, without you actively seeking alternative, body-positive options, it is more than likely going to be filled with Rosie Popes for miles. It's *not* that her body is bad, it's just that it doesn't represent the whole picture. If we want our media feeds to represent real life (and ultimately show us that our body isn't strange, weird, or awful), we need to go out and search for these images ourselves.

Once upon a time, when I was first exploring the concept of body positivity, I stumbled upon a list of body acceptance Tumblrs that kinda blew my mind. The diversity of bodies that I found was something that I hadn't ever seen or experienced before, and I couldn't look away. I was horrified, curious, fascinated, and enthralled all at the same time. I'll never forget an image a plus-size woman had posted of her and her thin boyfriend. They were taking a mirror selfie in the bathroom; she was wearing lingerie, her fat body unapologetically spilling out over her undies, and he was behind her, holding her in an intimate embrace. They were the essence of everything SUPER schmexy love looks like. A fat woman with a thin partner who was obviously attracted to her?

I couldn't process what I was seeing.

NEVER had I seen a picture of a fat person being sexy without it being the butt of a joke (fuck you, Ashley Madison), and never had I seen a sexy picture of a fat woman with a thin man. WAIT. YOU MEAN THIS HAPPENS IN REAL LIFE? It was the first time I was ever awakened to the fact that fat women had the option of dating whomever they wanted, and that all kinds of partners could (and do) find them sexy. The world simply refuses to show us such things, but Tumblr doesn't, and because of this my brain didn't really know what to do with the information. This was just one of thousands of images that rocked my world by showing diversity I had previously lived unaware of.

Unable to stop myself, I kept coming back for more. And the more bodies I saw, the more stretch marks I saw, the more skin shades I saw, the wider range of physical abilities I saw . . . the less strange they started to become. In fact, after a while, they started to seem normal to me. And then they *were* normal to me. The "off-screen" people around me suddenly seemed normal. I wasn't shocked by bodies in real life anymore; my "accidental gawking" was a thing of the past. My appreciation of all bodies grew, and I started to see the beauty in EVERYONE. And guess what? Eventually this turned into acceptance of myself, I shit you not. After a while I no longer cried when I looked in the mirror. I started to run my hands over my dips and curves without thinking I was a fuck-up. My body almost seemed . . . normal.

All from changing my Tumblr feed.

It might seem absurd to you (or not, in which case, YAY, go follow more Tumblrs!), but it's a perfect example of how easily our brains are conditioned. When we walk past magazine stands, go to the movie theater, and see advertisements on the subway walls, our brains are subconsciously receiving the message that there is a singular way to look that is considered "normal." Obviously, most of us won't be included in that definition. And whether we acknowledge it or not, that harmful message sits in our core and becomes internalized. Soon we are letting it dictate how we feel about ourselves. So let's reclaim our power and offer ourselves images that cover the diversity that exists in the real world, eh? We can do that so easily, it almost seems like a bummer not to.

If you you're the kind of person who tends to be skeptical of foul-mouthed fat chicks and needs some science to weigh in on the matter, I've gotcha covered. *PLOS ONE* (a scientific journal published by the Public Library of Science) featured a study called "Visual Diet Versus Associative Learning as Mechanisms of Change in Body Size Preferences," which sounds intimidating, so I'll rename it for you: Let's call it "We're More Easily Conditioned Than You Think, So Choose What You Look at Carefully." That, *or* "Change Your Tumblr, Change Your Life," duh.

The 2012 study noted that there seemed to be a discrepancy in what type of body (especially in regard to weight) Western culture prefers as compared to other parts of the world, a discrepancy that wasn't necessarily attributed to "biological attraction."[2]

Could it POSSIBLY be because we're force-fed one example of the perfect woman? Well, YEAH. So what happens when we change the body that is shown repeatedly? NPR covered the story as well:

> *Changing negative attitudes about body size might be as simple as changing what you see. When women in England were shown photos of plus-sized women in neutral gray leotards, they became more tolerant . . . "Showing them thin bodies makes them like thin bodies, more, and showing them fat bodies makes them like fat bodies more," says Lynda Boothroyd, a psychology researcher at Durham University in England, who led the study.*

Of course, because our conditioning runs as deep as Plato's thoughts (so, pretty damn deep), in that same study there was still weight bias among the participants—they "still preferred thinner-than-average bodies, but their preferences *did* move up or down depending on what they saw [emphasis mine]."[3] Meaning: We are retrainable. Our brains are re-conditionable. All is not lost, and nothing is fucked. If we actively feed ourselves visual proof of the diversity that exists in our world, we WILL learn to appreciate all bodies for what they are: A-OK. Awesome. Maybe even perfect.

Let me tell you about another real-life experience that has taught me that seeing multiple kinds of bodies is pretty critical for our own self-love.

If we actively feed ourselves visual proof of the diversity that exists in our world, we WILL learn to appreciate all bodies for what they are: A-OK. Awesome. Maybe even perfect.

Three years ago, I bravely (and impetuously) started my first large-scale photography project, which I called "The Body Image(s)." The purpose of the series was to highlight the individual beauty of all shapes and sizes without any digital corrections. While looking for models, I put out a call (secretly hoping for ten brave souls . . . I felt silly aiming so high) and was stunned by the overwhelmingly positive response. My inbox continued to fill day after day with emails from women who were enthusiastic about baring all so that their vulnerability could offer other women strength.

Over thirty women, ranging from rail thin to extra-extra-large, volunteered, and I soon had them naked on my bed doing all sorts of (what we would consider) "unflattering" poses. I would routinely ask them to hug their knees, touch their toes, or lean over while grabbing their tummies . . . and I could hardly believe it: ALL OF THEM HAD STOMACH ROLLS. Not one was exempt. Even my super-fabulous professional model, six-foot tall, and super-duper-thin friend Katy had rolls. Turns out, our skin needs to stretch in order for us to move, though photoshop fiends tend to forget that. Taking these images started to normalize my thoughts and dispel so many myths about what bodies look like when they are unclothed and unaltered.

A year later I recreated this shoot on an even larger scale by combining forces with a photographer named Liora K. We had seventy women volunteer to strip down to their skivvies (and some danced around fully nude!) in the name of body love and this book. I'll never forget the energy of that night, an evening spent in beautiful body solidarity with so many other courageous women. Breasts were bared, love was shared, lives were altered, and history was made. We dedicated our night to changing the world, a few asymmetrical nipples at a time. We were highly aware that these images needed to exist, and we knew that bombarding the Internet with them was important (review Chapter 6 for why). These images needed to be shared on Tumblr and every other platform to show that there is no wrong way to physically exist. Rolls, dimples, folds, color spots, stretch marks and more . . . all fucking beautiful.

A year later, we asked our city to join us again, and this time photos were taken of one hundred diverse women, and the images (collectively called "Expose") were shared on the web. "Expose" spread like wildfire online; it was covered by every inhabited continent in the world and translated into more languages than I can count. My own exposure to these bodies, both in the moment and while reviewing the images later, changed the way I saw bodies from then on. The worldwide popularity of "Expose" proved to me that we are all famished for proof that we are not alone in our body differences. When we normalize our differences they morph into similarities, and we can finally breathe a sigh of relief.

Because of these projects, I have become comfortable with and accustomed to seeing hundreds of boobs, thighs, stomachs, belly buttons, and glorious asses. Through these experiences, I started to note that not only do we have amazing similarities (rolls and cellulite!) but we also have fantastical differences. Each of us lives within a vessel that is uniquely ours and also perfectly "real." It reaffirmed for me that I was okay, scars, flab, rolls, body hair, and all. Maybe a DIY photo shoot with your friends is in order? Have I mentioned it's important to surround yourself with diverse images? Ten times already? Oh, good.

Now, I want to clarify that thing about turning off your TV and burning your magazines. Obviously there are some really harmful shows and magazines out there (I mean, women's magazines were

THE
**FAT
PEOPLE:**
do all the things!
CHALLENGE
✲

#6: FLY.

OH, THE MOST LOADED OF ALL THE
CHALLENGES. At this point in my life, I fly . . .
a LOT. Sometimes five or six trips a month. So,
not only do I break the rule that fat people shouldn't
fly, but I have also honed my fatty flying skills, and I wanna
share some tips with you that might make your next trip easier:

- **Use a seat belt extender:** Pretty sure you can
  squish your body into the tiny seats, but worry about
  clicking the seat belt? You're not alone. If you can't (the
  length varies), just ask for a seat belt extender. Many
  people just shout out, "I need that fat person buckle!"
  Or better yet, bring your own! They're available on
  Amazon and are TOTALLY bedazzleable.

- **Fly Southwest:** As of the printing of this book,
  Southwest Airlines has a "Customer of Size" policy.
  The idea behind it: You purchase two seats (to be sure
  they don't overbook), and after your flight you request
  a refund for the extra one. This means more worry-
  free room at no actual charge! I've heard this refund
  can take anywhere from a few days to a few months,
  but it does come. However, if fronting the money for
  two seats isn't possible for you, there is another way
  to make the system work for ya! For the super budget-
  friendly option, purchase one seat, and when you
  check in speak to the Southwest rep. Ask the rep if
  there is any extra room on the flight, and if so, request
  the "extra-fat-girl seat." Or call it the "Customer of Size
  seat"—they'll know what you mean. If there is room
  on the flight, this extra seat will be free, and they'll
  print out a special little boarding pass for you that says
  "Reserved." When you show your special Reserved

pass to the nice people at the gate, say, "Someone told me I should come up here so this can be included in preboarding." That someone would be me.

They shouldn't give you a hard time, but if they do, tell them Jes Baker says they should just do their job already, thankyouverymuch. When you preboard, you'll have your pick of seats. Sit down and place your Reserved pass next to you and *don't let anyone sit on it*. This is the part that sucks. People sometimes just don't get it. But fight 'em off, and choose your seats near the back of the plane so fewer people are likely to try to commandeer that space. Unless it has, at the last minute, become a full flight, you do not need to concede.

Honestly, it's a LOT of fucking work, but if you're on a five-hour (or more) flight and you don't want to be scrunched into the corner and elbowed by the middle person? It might be worth it. Know your options and that it is okay to take up space.

- **Pop a Xanax:** Or take something else to calm your nerves. If pills make you nervous, health food stores have options, so check them out. Flying is so difficult for some that they refuse to do it altogether; if you're tempted to stop flying but don't want to, try finding an aid to help you relax. I'm totally serious. It helps.

- **Be the last person on the plane:** Not on Southwest? Wait until the very end of the line to board so that when you walk on you can scout for any side-by-side empty seats. Too often we're afraid to "break the rules," but if everyone else has boarded and no one is sitting there, you can!

- **Acknowledge the elephant:** Y'know, the one in the room. Sitting down next to someone and it's uncomfortably tight? Mention it. Say, "Looks like we get to share a personal space bubble today!" A friend of mine often says, "Hope you like cuddling!" Whatever you need to say to take the edge off and settle in during the flight.

Your challenge: FLY, GODDAMNIT. Live that life. See the sights. Visit the people. Make it as enjoyable as you can, and fuck the people who have a problem with you. Fat people deserve to be able to fly and live a full, adventurous life, and there are even travel sites like travelabundantly.com that are dedicated to the cause!

designed to sell insecurity, for chrissakes). You know the ones I'm talkin' about: They leave you feeling sick to your stomach, like a failure, and hopeless about ever feeling good enough. I don't know if I need to say this, but ditch that shit. Anything that leaves you feeling less than is NOT worth your time. There are plenty of entertaining, enjoyable, and *non*-triggering TV shows, films (*The Hairdresser*!), and periodicals (*Bust* and *Bitch*!) that you can watch and read—you don't need to go completely off the grid. And of course, if you CAN get rid of anything with harmful messages (like *Pregnant with Heels*, shows that being thin and wealthy is sexy as hell), do. I'm just saying, "You don't have to cut an arm off, guys. Just a finger."

Because I'm nice like that.

Now, if we're going to remove anything from our lives, we have to replace it with something. This is rule numero uno if you're aiming for effective change. I've told you over and over again how important it is to shower your eyeballs with diverse images, so allow me to give you a starter list! Below you'll find a list of Tumblr accounts. Perhaps you'll find one that interests you, look at one of the images, click the original page where it came from, and find that you like that Tumblr, too! Build up your body-lovin' social media pages, and then give them a long, loving scroll every day. See what happens. I dare you.

Note: I'm definitely not responsible for the content on these sites, because, y'know, I have zero control over what they post. As of now, though, they seem pretty damn helpful! If you find one that doesn't work for you (many sites cover multiple subjects) or has gone rogue, that's cool. Skip it and find the ones that do work for you . . . there are a kajillion out there. These are just a few.

Regularize bodies; they don't all look the same. And if you're feeling like an overachiever, go back and read Chapter 6 and take some images of YOUR body. Start a Tumblr. Write a blog. Add to the wealth. Change the way we view bodies, one post at a time. And send me a link so I can share it, okay?

1. The Adipositivity Project (adipositivityproject.tumblr.com)

2. Beautiful Magazine (beautifulmagazine.tumblr.com)

3. The Body Love Conference (bodyloveconference.tumblr.com)

4. Body Posi (body-posi.tumblr.com)

5. Body Positivity for the Modern Man (bodypositivityforthemodernman.tumblr.com)

6. Chinese Fashion Lovers (chinesefashionlovers.tumblr.com)

7. Chubby Bunnies (chubby-bunnies.tumblr.com)

8. Chubby Cupcake (chubby-cupcake.tumblr.com)

9. Fat Art (fatart.tumblr.com)

10. Fat Can Dance (fatcandance.tumblr.com)

11. Fat People Art (fatpeopleart.tumblr.com)

12. Fat People of Color (fatpeopleofcolor.tumblr.com)

13. Fuck Yeah Body Image (fuckyeahbodyimage.tumblr.com)

14. Fuck Yeah Body Positivity (fuckyeahbodypositivity.tumblr.com)

15. Fuck Yeah Hard Femme (fuckyeahhardfemme.tumblr.com)

16. Fuck Yeah VBO (fyeahvbo.tumblr.com)

17. Guatemalan Rebel (guatemalanrebel.tumblr.com)

18. Halt the Body Hate (halt-the-body-hate.tumblr.com)

19. Hey Fat Chick (heyfatchick.tumblr.com)

20. His Black Dress (hisblackdress.tumblr.com)

21. Life Outside the Binary (lifeoutsidethebinary.com)

22. I Love Fat (ilovefat.tumblr.com)

23. Lotsa Lipstick (lotsalipstick.tumblr.com)

24. The Love Yourself Challenge (theloveyourselfchallenge.tumblr.com)

25. The Militant Baker, obvs (themilitantbaker.tumblr.com)

26. Natural Bods (naturalbods.tumblr.com)

27. Old Time Fatties (oldtimefatties.tumblr.com)

28. Plus Size Belly Dance (plussizebellydance.tumblr.com)

29. Queer Bodies Are (queerbodies.tumblr.com)

30. Redefining Body Image (redefiningbodyimage.tumblr.com)

31. Sex and Body Positive (bodypositivesexpositive.tumblr.com)

32. A Thick Girl's Closet (athickgirlscloset.tumblr.com)

33. Thou Shalt Love Thyself (thoushaltlovethyself.tumblr.com)

34. Transgender Revolution (stuffchrissylikes.tumblr.com)

35. Your Life in Design (www.yourlifeindesign.com)

BODY LOVE AND DISABILITIES:
INTERSECTIONS OF IDENTITY
SHANNA KATZ KATTARI, M.ED, ACS
OF SHANNAKATZ.COM

Among the similarities between being fat and being disabled, the most obvious to me is the way others talk about people in these groups, as if there is something wrong with being fat, or having disabilities. **Spoiler alert: There isn't anything wrong with either.**

In high school, when I'd go shopping at the mall with friends, I would come out of the fitting room and say something about how a certain item fit, that I didn't like how I looked in it, or that it was too tight for my fat ass. As in, my ass that was fat. Every time, my friends' automatic response was, "No, you're not fat! You're _____!" Fill in the blank with "pretty," "beautiful," "gorgeous"; you name a positive adjective around beauty, and it was said. The issue was that I *was* fat, *and* I was pretty/beautiful/gorgeous. For me, it wasn't an either/or situation, but given the way society views fatness, even when my friends were trying to be supportive they were reinforcing that fat was not okay.

Fast-forward a few years. After having several knee surgeries for my osteoarthritis, and finally being diagnosed with severe chronic migraines and fibromyalgia, I was ecstatic to have the terminology around being disabled that I could identify with. (Note: some people prefer to be referred to as a person with a disability—always ask people what their preference is!) However, I was soon replaying scenes of my high school shopping drama. One of my partners, upon hearing of my frustration with the limitations caused by my disabilities, responded by saying, "You're not disabled; you're perfect for everything I could want from you." Again, here was the assumption that I could either be disabled or a perfect partner, but I certainly could not be both.

Being both fat and disabled, I constantly face messages from the world at large that not only am I outside the norm, but because I'm fat and disabled I cannot be beautiful, or develop healthy relationships. Those are some pretty sad messages to be getting over and over and over again. Add to this the trope of fat people being lazy; I've been told to "just take the stairs" more times than I can count. While no one should ever have to experience that, I physically *cannot* take the stairs. I was fat before I was disabled, and I am fat now that I am disabled . . . and while I enjoy a lazy "Caturday" here and there, my productiveness is in no way correlated to my body.

Finding the disability community was an amazing experience for me; it was similar to my experience discovering the body love community. Finally, people celebrated me for all of me—including my size and disabilities, instead of in spite of them. More importantly, these communities supported ME in loving ME for who I am, period.

When we talk about loving our bodies, we mean loving YOUR OWN body. This means bodies that have four limbs, bodies that have no limbs, and everything in between. This means bodies that have chronic pain, bodies that need to spend the whole day in bed, bodies that use adaptive devices. Bodies that have metal joints, screws, bone grafts, skin grafts, plates, plastics—anything. Bodies that have every level of sight, every level of hearing, every level of mobility.

This is not to say that people with disabilities have to always love their bodies and how they are feeling at any given point in time; every person of every ability has moments of frustration, anger, and disillusion. No one should ever feel that they have to put on a fake smile through pain, or through assholes making comments about ability issues. Everyone has the right to have space to love their bodies, and to have moments when they don't.

On the other hand, it is important to normalize disabilities and impairments. This means creating spaces that are accessible to those of all abilities; featuring people with disabilities on TV and in movies, and books; designing mannequins that reflect the diversity of abilities that exist in society. It also means checking our language: When you use words like "lame," "crazy," "insane," "invalid," "dumb," "deaf," you are reinforcing "ableism," which means valuing people without disabilities over those who have disabilities. Asking people if they are deaf when they ask you to repeat something, or calling a situation crazy (when what you mean is ridiculous or out of control) is one way to police the bodies of people who ARE deaf or have a mental health diagnosis.

How can we in the body love movement make sure people with disabilities are included?

- Make sure people with disabilities (visible AND invisible) are included in our photo shoots, artwork, performances, books (like this one!), and other media. Sometimes this means extra work up front, but it is so worth it to offer images that truly represent the community.

- Be aware of the language you use. Rather than having an event with a "crazy cat lady" theme, consider a cat-lovers' party instead. Don't talk about people who police bodies as being lame; call them out as hurtful or insensitive. The fact that a store only carries certain sizes isn't dumb; it's ridiculous and sizeist. Say what you mean!

- Offer sign language interpreters at body love events, and include information about event accessibility on flyers and event promotional materials. Transcribe speeches and podcasts after the fact (volunteers can do this) so people with limited hearing can participate, and use subtitles in any videos. Put aside quiet space for folks who may experience sensory overstimulation, and consider offering scent-free zones for those who are limited by the scents worn by others.

- Recognize intersectionality. People with disabilities are fat, slim, svelte, zaftig, tall, short, and everything in between. Disabled folks are straight, lesbian, gay, bisexual, queer, asexual, pansexual, and questioning their orientation. People of color have disabilities too, as do transgender and gender nonconforming individuals. Don't make people choose between identities.

- Include disabled folks as part of the movement. This doesn't mean bringing them in at the last minute, or parading one person around as your token disabled friend. Ensure planning committees and work groups are accessible and open to all folks, and offer topics that are relevant to—and even center workshops on—disability-related issues.

Not sure if your event, flyer, or art project is inclusive, or want help with next steps? Just ask. Google is a wonderful thing for finding information online, and when you put out a call online asking for help making something more accessible and inclusive, people will usually recognize that support is needed and give you some ideas to help propel you forward!

It's so easy to fall into the trap of self-loathing. I don't always love my chubby tummy, my squishy butt, my ever shrinking boobs . . . but then my knees and hips ache and everything connected with my head, neck, and shoulders results in the screeching pain of migraines, and on those days there isn't a single part of my body that doesn't hurt. How do I love a body that does this to me? The ever-changing combination of meds I take has resulted in epic weight loss, then intense weight gain, mood changes, sleeplessness, chronic exhaustion, frustration, nausea, dizziness, and even a series of kidney infections. My disabilities impact my body in so many ways, and sometimes that makes it hard for me to love me.

But hot damn if my body isn't amazing despite all that. I've had four knee surgeries now; I'm part bionic and part cadaver grafts, and my body has accepted these invasions and welcomed them. I have discovered the brilliance of playing and working out in water; when I find something that works, whether it is a new medication, massage, essential oil, dietary change, chocolate, or stretch, I celebrate my body being open to constantly experiencing new things. When I gather with my "crip" family (note: "Crip" is a term that has been reclaimed by many disabled individuals, but isn't a word to just go slinging around willy-nilly), we laugh and cry and celebrate and get out frustrations and get creative and "MacGyver" shit; we adapt things; we find ways we can not only engage with a world that actively discourages our bodies, but also ways to take that world by storm. I am not telling you that all you have to do is close your eyes and click your heels together and magically you'll love your body, but even in the midst of hurt and pain and lack of access, remember how hard your body (and your mind and your heart) are working to exist in a world that doesn't want to believe that people like us are beautiful, handsome, dapper, sassy, fierce, successful, brilliant, amazing, and self-satisfied. But we know we are. Crip love.

*

100% of humans have brains: mental health support is for everyone

[CHAPTER EIGHT]

F act: 100% of humans have brains.

I know I'm seriously stating the most obvious thing right now, but bear with me. There's more to this than meets the eye. I promise.

In the U.S., the new common statistic is that one in five adults—about 61.5 million Americans—experiences mental illness in a given year.[1] That's 20 percent of us who are dealing with some sort of brain disorder. If you and I and everyone else who reads this book were all sitting in a group and I count off, pointing to each of us in turn, it goes: One, two, three, four, you. One, two, three, four, you. That's A LOT of people! And those are just the mental illnesses that are diagnosed; that leaves out all the others who (1) don't know what mental illness is or looks like, (2) are afraid to seek help because of the enormous stigma attached to it, or (3) don't know how to access or navigate the support available.

Well, here's my statistic (and that of many other professionals): **One hundred percent of adults have brains, and zero percent of them work perfectly.** Therefore, while it's commonly thought that only the 20 percent of people (those who are clinically diagnosed) are in need of mental health resources and help, I propose that 100 percent of us could use mental health support and assistance.

And **there's nothing wrong with that.**

That's a fact, not just opinion.

Before we delve any further, I'm sure you're wondering why the fuck I feel so comfortable talking about all of this. To give you a frame of reference, I've worked in several roles in the behavioral health/mental health world: as a psych-social rehabilitation specialist, a behavioral health technician (or BHT), a certified recovery support specialist (CRSS), and a mental health educator.

As a *psych-social rehabilitation specialist,* I coached those with serious mental illnesses through their recovery in a real work environment so they could ultimately gain independent employment.

A *BHT* works with individuals with a mental illness in various settings. This person has at least four years of experience through work or school and applies this knowledge wherever they are employed.

A *CRSS* is someone who is trained and certified to coach people with mental illnesses and has been diagnosed with a mental illness or substance use disorder themselves. These specialists are also known as peer mentors or peer navigators. Recovery support specialists are highly sought after and have been ever since researchers discovered that one of the most successful forms of rehabilitation available is working with someone who has also gone through recovery. This is changing the way we view individuals with diagnoses, and it's fucking rad.

As a *mental health educator,* I worked for an agency that supported me in creating and implementing a state-funded curriculum designed to train adults with mental illness on how to prepare to become CRSSs/peer mentors.

I left behavioral health recently after juggling full-time work, my blog, speaking engagements, conference planning, and a book deadline, all of which led to complete and total burnout (it was brutal!). Will I go back? Perhaps someday. But only time will tell.

But for now, when it comes to this book, I'd like to be clear: I am not a psychiatrist, therapist, or any other licensed professional. Eventually, perhaps, but for now I'm speaking to you as someone who has lived a lot, seen a lot, taught a lot, read a lot, and trained a lot, and I want to share some real brain talk with you.

Because real brain talk is the best kind.

This book is mostly about bodies, but if we talk about bodies and social impact we gotta also talk about brains. Pretending that the body and the brain are not inextricably connected is kind of silly.

By living in a world that constantly tries to squash our self-esteem, all the while telling us to rise up and defeat the odds, we're put in a position that severely impacts our mental health. This takes a SIGNIFICANT toll on our self-esteem and mental coping skills. Combine that pressure with the fact that our brains are never 100 percent perfect, and, well . . . we all need some brain support, and there is nothing wrong with that, no matter what anyone else says.

Now, I've done a LOT of personal recovery work over the years. What has that meant for me? It has meant being in intensive therapy since 2008. Trying *a lot* of medications in order to find the ones that work perfectly for me. Building a support system that is balanced. Finding the foods that feed my brain appropriately. Finding a physical outlet that I don't hate (besides sex, wink wink). All that and developing coping mechanisms I can use every day. My recovery plan is pretty airtight and has allowed me to be a successful, productive, and busy lady, but does that mean mental issues never surface? HELLLLLLLLL. NO.

I still have days in which I (seemingly for no reason) crash and fucking burn. It's part of the human condition, and even though I hate it, my brain has the capability to break down as all of our brains occasionally do. Which has led me to ask myself, *What to do, Jes, when things get too hard?*

I have some simple suggestions for you (and me) that can make daily brain issues—which are different from serious mental illnesses—a little bit easier to deal with.

Option 1: Create a "five-legged support system."

In my CRSS training, I learned that the best support system is like a five-legged stool. If you have just one "leg" of support, your recovery topples. Same with two. Three can balance, but if one breaks you're SOL. Four is pretty stable, but again, lose a couple and you're flat on your ass. Five legs allow you to remain stable even if a leg or two were to disappear. So what do these "legs" look like? They can be anything that supports you. For me, many of the legs are people. My mom. My boy. Close friends. My therapist. And sometimes support legs can be actions like dance class. There is no shame in this game; we all need support to get through this tough thing called life. So find those five or more legs that work for you, and then *lean* on them.

Other potential legs of support: Creating art. Calling a crisis line. Writing. Making music. Reading inspirational books. Making a list of things you're grateful for. Your favorite form of exercise. Cooking a delicious meal. And perhaps some of the actions listed in number 2.

Option 2: Make a "hard-day plan" *before* you have a hard day.

It's really useful to create a list of things that make you instantly feel better for those days where you're in a downward spiral. The idea being: When you can't function, go to your already-made list, pick one thing, and just do it. Ideally, after doing one (or three) of these items, your brain feels a little better and allows you to continue on with life. The best part? Lots of them can be totally free. Here are some that work for me:

- **Ride my bicycle around downtown.** I hate a lot of forms of exercise, but bicycling is an exception. Endorphins are magic. This gets them going instantly.

- **Get coffee at a local cafe and sit on the outside patio.** Twinkle lights and peppermint iced tea soothe my soul.

- **Turn on music and dance with my cats.** They hate it, but it does wonders for me.

- **Take myself on a movie theater date.** Yep. This.

- **Shower.** As simple as that. A physical reset button.

- **Call Mom.** It could be anyone for you, whoever is part of your support system.

- **Peruse Tumblr.** For some reason, my Tumblr feed is the perfect blend of empowering and fucking hilarious.

- **Give myself a makeovah.** I rarely take the time to put makeup on, do up my hair, and preen like I did when I was younger, but I still love it. "Victory rolls," falsies, red lipstick . . . the whole gamut.

- **Have a salad bar hour.** This actually gives me several forms of self-care: both the get-out-of-the-house part *and* the nutritional-boost part. I love going to the co-op and buying an eclectic basketful of spinach salad ingredients. I follow it up by going home and making a point to be mindful and enjoy creating my masterpiece. And then I devour it with garlic bread, of course.

- **Write.** Whatever, wherever. Get it out of your body and brain and onto paper. The act of writing got me through college (Xanga, anyone?) and still continues to be a cathartic release for me.

- **Make a gratitude list.** I can actually demonstrate this one right now:

   I'm grateful for being born into many opportunities. I'm grateful for my three fluffy roommates. I'm grateful for my education. I'm grateful to have a body that heals itself and lets me pursue my dreams. I'm grateful for Bath and Body Works lotions. I'm grateful that I live in the same city as my family. I'm grateful that I write online. I'm grateful for bagels. I'm grateful for ending up on a path that allows me to love myself. I'm grateful for polka dots and stripes. I'm grateful for blooming orange trees. I'm grateful for air conditioning. I'm grateful for free speech. I'm grateful for being loved.

Making a gratitude list helps me every time.

- **Spend the day browsing at a bookstore.** Get on the bus, get in your car, or walk to a bookstore so you can grab a stack of books and read. Preferably forever.

- **Have a greasy-spoon breakfast and read the newspaper.** I don't know what it is about this combination that makes life worth living . . . but I'm not going to fuck with it. It's perfect.

- **Have sex**. With your fingers, with your shower head, with your vibrator, with your partner, with a lover . . . get those good vibes going, stat!

I would suggest you make your own list . . . right now. Like *now* now. Take the hard part of thinking about what to do out of the equation when you're next in a rut. Write it down or print it out and put it on your fridge or in your journal—wherever it's visible and easy to find. And the next time you feel like shit and all looks dismal, peek at your sheet and force yourself to try just one. You are your own best resource, baby. Put yourself to good use.

Option 3: When you're actually *having* one of those hard days, work this diagram. I'm serious.

I created this diagram and process while teaching students how to prepare to become a CRSS. It was an exceptionally rough day, and I made an executive decision to use the shitty day as a learning experience and ditched the lesson plan altogether. The thing we learned

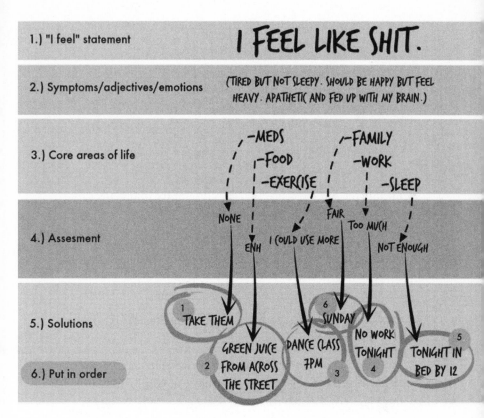

1.) "I feel" statement	**I FEEL LIKE SHIT.**
2.) Symptoms/adjectives/emotions	(TIRED BUT NOT SLEEPY. SHOULD BE HAPPY BUT FEEL HEAVY. APATHETIC AND FED UP WITH MY BRAIN.)
3.) Core areas of life	—MEDS —FOOD —EXERCISE —FAMILY —WORK —SLEEP
4.) Assesment	NONE EHH I COULD USE MORE FAIR TOO MUCH NOT ENOUGH
5.) Solutions / 6.) Put in order	¹TAKE THEM ²GREEN JUICE FROM ACROSS THE STREET ³DANCE CLASS 7PM ⁶SUNDAY ⁴NO WORK TONIGHT ⁵TONIGHT IN BED BY 12

that day in class (and that I always try to remember) is that we already have ALL the answers, and we *can* find solutions all on our own; it's just a matter of asking ourselves the right questions. This process borrows from cognitive behavioral therapy (CBT), and will hopefully help the next time you have a day full of not-awesome.

Use a whiteboard, use a scrap of paper, whatever you need. Here is how it goes:

1. Write an "I feel" statement. Yes, write. It's so amazing what the commitment to paper (or whiteboard) can do for problem solving. WRITE LIKE YOU MEAN IT. That day I felt "like shit." Yes, I really wrote that in class, and it was well received; we all feel that way sometimes. My "I feel" was simple and straightforward. That's it. Done!

2. Underneath it, describe what that looks like: symptoms, adjectives, emotions—things you want to shout aloud. I felt tired, but not sleepy. Like I *should* (ugh, don't ever *should* on yourself!) be happy but instead I just felt heavy. I felt apathetic and fed up with my fucked-up brain for not giving me a break, and for just plain cramping my style. FUCK YOU, NEURONS!!!

3. Identify the core influencers of your life. The big things, the items that most affect the way you feel. Many people have a list of ten-plus things, and that's totally cool. That day I focused on the major areas: medication, nutrition/food, family, exercise, sleep, and work. Get it down. This is what you're going to work through in the next part, so make them thorough.

4. Assess those motherfuckers. Examine the components you listed in step 3. Are you caring for each area properly? Can you improve? What role are these areas playing in your day-to-day—positive or negative? Is there something that needs to be tweaked? Answer these honestly. On that particular shitty day I hadn't taken my medication in two days (that was a DUH, YOU'RE NOT FEELING WELL factor). I was eating "well enough," but not superdeeduper great. I could have used a high dose of exercise that day. I wasn't sleeping. At all. My eighty-six-hour work weeks had me fucking burned out. So there. I was basically needing improvement in all areas. No wonder I felt like shit!

   Now, there *is* the potential that some of your core items are going well (others had partners, house maintenance, creative outlets, that were helping them), AND THAT'S AMAZING. KEEP THAT SHIT UP (and note it)! And then proceed to number 5.

5. Solution-ize. What can you do TODAY (you're feeling crappy *today*, aren't you?) to rectify some of those core issues? Be reasonable, and gentle with yourself. Do NOT try and overhaul

your life right now; that will be ineffective and will inevitably cause more overwhelm. Instead, create a simple and doable action plan, steps you can take to improve things, and if you can't do them all today, put a select few in the immediate future! Having positive steps to look forward to taking can ease some of the immediate stress.

That day I decided to leave the class right then and there and take my medication. This step was critical to my well-being, and if I didn't do it then I'd likely forget. So, check! I was already making progress. Nutrition: I needed more greens. A trip to the juice bar across the street during lunch was in order. I also needed an endorphin boost, bad; I decided to go to a dance class that night, one I don't normally attend, and fix that shit STAT.

Also, I wasn't sleeping. And when I don't sleep I am easily overwhelmed, angered, grumpy, and depressed. STOP NOT SLEEPING, JES, IT'S SMOTHERING YOUR FIRE. Okay, Self. I promise to be in bed by midnight, come hell or high water. And lastly . . . work. Sigh. The work days leading up to class had zapped my energy and glossed over my eyes. Though my work was positive, I needed to take a break from it all that night. My new plan was dance class and then a movie night with cheap wine and a friend. The piles of *to-do*'s would be there tomorrow! Be as detailed as possible in your solution-izing (I wrote down when I was going to do those things, even put that my dance class was at seven o'clock).

Now literally circle those motherfuckers; you're winning at life!

6. Put them all in order. Whenever we're in any sort of crisis stage, we revert back to a toddler mentality. True story. We need things to be clearly outlined, in order, and easy to follow. Use this diagram to give yourself organized instructions to make it through. Because you were *so detailed* in your solution stage (riiiiiiiiiiiiiight?), it should be a snap to organize your solutions into an action plan starting right now! THEN you can execute

them without hurting your brain or feeling overwhelmed or wondering what you should do next. I KNOW it sounds so basic it hurts, but it's really important, and you'd be surprised how often we forget to do this.

I'm not exaggerating when I say that after completing my diagram I felt immediately better. Something about facing issues head on, having an action plan to follow, and knowing there were reasons for why I felt the way I did really helped solidify my core. I also assisted three students with this process—their diagrams were all drastically different, but they all had the same positive outcomes. Now, a year later, comments and emails from around the world confirm the same. Kick-ass to say the least. Keep this one in your back pocket!

Option 4: Treat your brain like a car.

My friend Allison, who is my "brain buddy"—we have long conversations about mental health issues, and I can call her in the middle of the night when I'm in crisis—has one of the most brilliant analogies for mental self-care that I've ever heard.

She says our brains are like cars: Some people are born with a 2015 Lexus and some are born with a 1978 Yugo. Me? I was born with a car that has lots of quirks that breaks down... a *lot*. These "special cars" need extra care, and require forethought before taking them on long trips. It's not bad, it's not good; it just is what it is. Okay, fine, it might be a little inconvenient. But since we have no choice about which car we were born with, the only thing we can do for ourselves is learn the best way to take care of them so those babies stay on the road lookin' fly.

But this still begs the question: What do we do when we take care of it just so, and it STILL breaks down on the side of the road? Well, we go through the following checklist and find out what we need to get it back up and running.

THE CAR CARE (A.K.A. BRAIN CARE) CHECKLIST

☐ **Be sure you have enough gas.** Our bodies are definitely machines, and they need fuel at all times. It sounds basic, but sometimes I forget that. One of the first questions Allison often asks me is, "When was the last time you ate?" I also like to check in with myself about *what* I've been eating, making sure I'm eating the right things to keep me going.

☐ **Recharge your battery.** Another unappreciated self-care item: SLEEP. It's something that many of us who teach recovery strategies harp on often, er . . . I mean, strongly suggest. We must must *must* let ourselves reset and recover from our days. As someone who is accustomed to eighty-hour weeks, I have to remind myself of this often.

☐ **Always keep those jumper cables on hand.** These are the little actions that give us that quick, happy boost when our battery dies, when we "break down." Each person's jumper cables look a little different. Getting that jump-start could come from reading an inspiring book. Hopping in the shower. Going for a walk. Watching a movie. Getting dolled up. Make a list like the one you made in (or check your list from) Option 2 above.

☐ **Get some friends to help you push.** Remember that five-legged stool of supports we talked about in Option 1? USE THAT! Friends and others in your support system will help you get off the side of the road when you simply can't push the car by yourself. They're there to help you when you get stuck, and if someone's arms get tired, there are others who will be able to come take a turn!

☐ **Make an appointment with your mechanic.** SO CRITICAL. Many times, we simply need professional help—people who are trained, educated, and outside the situation so they have a clear perspective. It could be a therapist, counselor, doctor, or psychiatrist. Allow yourself to ask for professional help if you need it. These people exist for a damn good reason.

But still, you can do all the "right things" and your car might break down. Maybe your car is extra clunky like mine. If that's the case, let me make this clear: The resting state of your car is NOT your fault. Feeling guilty or shameful about breaking down will get us nowhere. All we can do is learn how to tune it up to the best of our ability, and, when we max out our skills, use the resources around us.

And as my goddamnwonderful boyfriend recently reminded me: "Even high-performance and super-sexy race cars break down, babe." *Oh yeah!* I realized. And they need an entire TEAM to put them back on the road.

Option 5: Put your self-care FIRST.

If there's only one thing you leave with from this chapter, I hope it is: **Take care of yourself above all else**. It isn't greedy. It isn't selfish. It's absolutely necessary, and this concept can translate into every part of your life. Author and feminist activist Audre Lorde has a quote that begins with, "Caring for myself is not self-indulgence, it is self-preservation." And I say: AMEN.

Self-care can include anything you need to keep going. Cooking. Exercise. Medical care. Setting boundaries. Ridding your life of toxic people. Cultivating positive friendships. Sleep. Getting counseling. Journaling. Reading. Meditating. Carving out "you time." Any actions that help your physical, mental, and emotional well-being. Whatever it is that makes you feel whole and happy . . . do more of that.

I learned the importance of self-care quickly once I started working in mental health. Previously I had worked as a full-time baker, which included long days of heavy labor on my feet doing mass production. It was not sedentary work by any means. But during my first week doing job coaching for adults with mental illness on how to make a single batch of cookies, I left ten times as exhausted, after producing ten times LESS product. I couldn't figure out why I was working so much less but feeling it so much more. How does that even happen?

The reason was a thing called compassion fatigue, and it's important enough to warrant entire books written about it.

Compassion fatigue is a common occurrence that happens to caretakers who work with individuals in emotionally taxing situations, like I was doing. Caretakers of any kind are professionally encouraged to up the ante when it comes to taking care of themselves so they can survive and avoid burnout.

I would argue that there is some element of compassion fatigue for everyone, even if the source of their paychecks doesn't fall under the umbrella of "caretaker." Parents, those who are members of families, people who are friends to others . . . I'm looking at you.

And compassion fatigue is really common in people who are taught that caring for others is far more important than taking care of themselves. Which is completely and totally backwards. When you put your well-being before anything else, you have more energy, space, and heart to assist others. It's the only way it really works.

We ALL could use a little more self-care.

Comprende?

Now on to the topic of serious mental illness.

I'm going to skip the clinical jargon and go for the super-simple explanation: A serious mental illness is a brain disorder that highly impairs an individual's life. Serious mental illnesses affect 9.6 million of us every year in the U.S., so collectively they impact our lives on a monumental level.[2]

A lot of people wonder why I use the word "illness" to describe mental disorders. The simple reason is that I believe a person with mental illness actually *has an illness* (defined by Merriam-Webster as "a specific condition that prevents your body or mind from working normally: a sickness or disease").[3] It's not a fabricated nuisance. It's not something that can be wished away.

We don't culturally shame someone who has, for example, a brain tumor, yet we often marginalize those who are trying to cope with, say, bipolar disorder. Writer Susie Campbell answers the question, "What if we treated every illness the way we treat mental illness?" in a cartoon she created with that title, where her characters say things like "I'm getting very tired of this *cancer* of yours."[4]

If you're more comfortable with calling it a "brain glitch" or "biological deficiency," by all means DO! I believe even using terms like those could help us get closer to talking about the true nature of mental illness. I plan on using that term until the stigma is removed and those with diagnoses are given the support, care, and resources they need. Y'feel?

Now, a serious mental illness is not determined by the NAME of the diagnosis, but rather the intensity with which it affects the person's life, which can vary widely, even for the same person over a period of time. How can we measure this? Back in the day, one of the tools clinicians would use to categorize illnesses was called the Global Assessment of Functioning, or the GAF scale. While the GAF scale has since been replaced by other tools, it's still a great way to clearly demonstrate the many shades of mental illness and how it can affect a person's life. While the tool itself may be outdated, the concept is not, and it has forever changed the way I view mental illness in a positive way.

Imagine a ruler, with marks for every centimeter going from 1 to 100, each of which correlates to how much your brain is helping or hindering you at the moment. The mark at number 1 indicates you're having a really hard time functioning at all, and 99 means your brain is working totally in your favor and nothing could be better! I refuse to use the 100 mark, because I think no one's brain can be flawless, and I like to establish this up front so I don't end up having a real-talk sit-down with someone that starts with "So, about that *bullshit perfection standard* . . . "

So, looking at that ruler and starting from 1 and moving to the right, **1–10** indicates persistent danger of severely hurting oneself or others, *or* persistent inability to maintain minimal personal hygiene, *or* a serious suicidal act with clear expectation of death. Marks **31–40** would mean some impairment in perception of reality or ability to communicate, *or* major impairment in work, school, family relations, judgment, or mood. In the range of **61–70**, a person might show some mild symptoms like depressed mood or insomnia, *or* some difficulty in functioning socially or at school, but generally would be able to function fairly well and have some meaningful interpersonal relationships. Toward the end of the ruler in the **81– 90** range, symptoms are absent or minimal; you might have mild anxiety before an exam, but otherwise you're basically "functioning" in all areas, are interested and involved in a wide range of activities, and are generally satisfied with life, with no more than everyday problems or concerns.

Why do I love this concept so much? Several reasons: It shows the layers and shades of gray in mental health. We as humans can get so stuck in how a diagnosis separates us from others, but the GAF scale forces us to look at the larger picture and remember that mental health is just a continuum, and we're all on it somewhere. And y'know what? There's a chance that at one point in our lives we might be one number, and another time we'll land somewhere completely different. This tool is just a starting point to assess ourselves and see what we might need to do to move toward the right side of the ruler, if we can.

The shame, guilt, and stigma we place on someone with a serious mental illness is a bunch of baloney. There was a long-running joke while I was in CRSS training that if you highlighted every disorder listed in the *Diagnostic and Statistical Manual of Mental Disorders* that you noticed in yourself at one time or another, you'd just have one big yellow book.

We all have some percentage of neurological deficiency and we all fall somewhere in between 1 and 99. Which simply means we're all in need of resources, just some more than others.

Y'follow?

If you are someone who identifies with having a mental illness—wherever it falls on the spectrum—I want to make sure you know something.

Your mental illness is not your fault.

Didja hear that? Again: **Your mental illness is not your fault.**

Here is why it's not your fault: We are a product of our chemistry and the sum of our collective experiences, and we cannot fully control either. We are born into our bodies, and our biological makeup dictates a lot of how we see the world. As adults now, *we can* choose how our life progresses, but of course nature and nurture have set us up with the tools we have. This includes our body issues.

My point: It's not necessary or helpful to feel guilt and shame about a neurological condition that is out of your control. That's all. So release yourself from that shit, and maybe you'll be able to focus your energy on what you want to see happen now.

It can be tricky to find help, and even if you make the difficult decision to seek it, you're going to have to commit yourself to a journey. With serious mental illnesses, medication is often necessary to lift us out of the rut we're in. It's okay; don't subscribe to whatever stigma you think exists about medication. Once you're *able to get out of bed*, you can then work on your recovery through activities like therapy, groups, exercise, et cetera. But you can't do any of those things if you're not able to leave your house. Medication is a simply a tool that helps you function.

If you think you may need a therapist but have anxiety about talking to someone in person (I prefer a real live person, but that's totally understandable), check out Talkspace (www.talkspace.com) where you can chat anonymously with one of more than two hundred therapists.

THE
**FAT
PEOPLE:**
do all the things!
CHALLENGE
*

#7: WEAR A BIKINI.

You've probably read this before: "How to have a bikini body: Have a body. Put on a bikini." It's that simple.

Fortunately, in the last few years fatkinis (bikinis in fat people sizes!) have not only become available, but they're something people love to wear. I recommend you jump on this boat. Check out companies like ModCloth, Forever 21 Plus, ASOS Curve, Lane Bryant, Monif C., and Walmart (yes, Walmart), and see if they have anything you like. And if you're reading this book ten years after it's published and are wondering where to find current swimwear, check out the relevant plus-size bloggers. They always know where to go.

Your challenge: If you're into it, suck it up (NOT in) and wear the goddamn bikini already! Don't look for a *Sports Illustrated* model in the mirror; look for you. Know you're enough. That you get to rock it too. And then go have some fun!

If you don't have the funds to get professional help, I would recommend using the services available through your local government agency. I'll be real with you, though: You may need an extreme amount of patience to navigate government networks, but it can be worth it. Just know that you're entitled to good care, and if you don't receive it, you're also entitled to ask for a new clinician. You are your own best advocate, so ask questions; ask for what you need; bring a list if you're afraid you'll forget the important stuff. Request a peer support specialist or recovery support specialist, if the agency has these available. These professionals will know how the system works and can help you get the resources you need.

If you've tried the coping skills I've outlined above and still find yourself in crisis, call a hotline. It may feel scary, but try to allow yourself to ask for support—people who staff these hotlines are trained to help people like you at a time like this. I've listed here a few that might be helpful.

1. National Hopeline Network (crisis hotline)
   1-800-SUICIDE // 1-800-784-2433

2. National Suicide Prevention Lifeline
   1-800-273-TALK // 1-800-273-8255

3. Suicide and Crisis Hotline and Adolescent Crisis
   Intervention and Counseling Nineline
   1-800-999-9999

4. Adolescent Suicide Hotline
   1-800-621-4000

5. Suicide Prevention—the Trevor Lifeline
   "Specializing in gay and lesbian youth suicide prevention"
   1-866-488-7386

6. The Trans* Lifeline
   "Dedicated to the wellbeing of transgender people"
   U.S.: 877-565-8860
   Canada: 877-330-6366

7. Mental Health Crisis Hotline
   1-800-273-TALK // 1-800-273-8255

8. Help Finding a Therapist
   1-800-THERAPIST // 1-800-843-7274

One more thing: There is a common misconception that suffering from a mental illness means you're broken or weak. On this, I call bullshit. Acknowledging that you have a biological imbalance is one of the bravest things that you can do: It is a sign of *strength*, not weakness. So you have that extra barrier and you STILL get up in the morning? Baby, that makes you miraculous. You deserve a standing ovation and a certificate for your stunning survival. You are my hero. Never give up.

I sure as hell won't.

UNDERSTANDING THE ROLE OF
CONFLICT AND BODY IMAGE IDENTITY
KIMBERLY A. PEACE, MSW OF
KIM–PEACE.COM

Self-loathing is at epidemic rates and is an alarming social problem today, especially pertaining to body image and self-perception. Tragically, this is strongly rooted in, and perpetuated by, mainstream society on a collective and individual basis. How did we get to this place? What are the underlying motives for creating a system of defined "beauties" and "non-beauties"? What causes a group or an individual to discriminate against others and cause harm, simply for looking different? Further, what phenomenon occurs within ourselves that allows us to accept another's negative perception of us? These questions frame an interesting debate.

Consider that on an individual basis, when someone identifies a person as unworthy of acceptance, unattractive, less than intelligent, or deserving of invisibility, a significant disconnection occurs. Prejudice, hatred, and injurious judgment often result from this type of interaction, and dehumanization occurs. One individual then claims power over another by labeling that person, creating a false sense of superiority, and distinguishing the other person's difference as an indication he or she is "less than." Social Darwinism, an evolutionary theory, describes the unwarranted justification of this privilege taken by some members of society. It is thought that natural selection based on biological traits is a viable measurement of who is "worthy" and who is "not worthy" in our society. Social Darwinists postulate that because humans are a product of nature and conflict, only the strongest, most intelligent, most beautiful (by American ethnocentric ideology) are considered acceptable. Any individual who does not seem to fit this mold is then viewed as destined to fail, and treated accordingly. Those individuals are defined as different, inherently inferior, and less deserving. Unfortunately, over time the recipients of such messaging may begin to accept this ideology and feel unacceptable, adopting behaviors that perpetuate this *internalized oppression* in their lives. They may begin to distrust themselves and their previous self-concept, and even loathe themselves. The result is that people who are judged in this way can, unknowingly, further fuel the power differential, which intensifies the dehumanization of all involved.

The underlying motives for perpetuating this type of interaction are multifaceted. Upon initial observation, *ignorance* plays a major role in discrimination. The idea that "you are different from me" may feel threatening to some. This lack of understanding seems to create *fear*. Specifically, fear of the unknown, fear of what outcomes may result from our differences. This fear creates a *disconnection* between individuals. This disconnection from one another can produce a strong reaction called psychological "reactance." Reactance is the motivational state aroused when a person perceives a threat to his or her own freedom, and feels a need to take action to regain a sense of control. In essence, someone who fears another person's differences may become verbally or physically violent toward the person. The "justification" for discrimination might include statements like, "You are fat and lazy," "You contribute nothing to society," "You cost taxpayers money for your health care," "You are skinny; you are weak," in an attempt to move away from the fear of difference and the discomfort it may have produced for this individual. Attempts may be made to coerce the other person into conforming and changing to match the status quo.

At this point, one is left with a choice to make: *Do I conform and try to change my body? Should I laugh it off and make fun of myself? Cry myself to sleep? Withdraw and feel numb? Battle the overwhelming fear that I might never belong?* These are common internal responses for the person who has been judged when trying to cope with the conflicts that arise over acceptance and body image identity. What can one do in the face of rejection? What are viable alternatives?

It becomes important, then, for all of us to find ways to stand up for our own and others' right to dignity and speak out in defense of justice in the world. How can we do this?

The **first step** is to recognize that conflict is inevitable. Embracing conflict with the will to create liberation can be a very powerful move. When we pursue personal freedom, we will inevitably be met with societal pushback based on what is deemed acceptable and what is not. Acknowledging the role of conflict in the potential to bring about positive change is vital.

Second, we have the opportunity to question the injustice or discrimination taking place. We can ask ourselves:

- Do I—or can I—believe in the inherent value of each person, regardless of our *commonalities or differences?*
- Can I respect others and myself for the individuals that we are?
- Do we all have the right to be ourselves, be safe, and feel accepted?

If we are unsure, then we can seek the ideas of others whom we trust and continue to question what society mandates. Take your time. Listen to others' experiences and think carefully about your own. What has been helpful for you, and what has been harmful?

Third, if we find that there are hurtful beliefs that permeate our lives, we can make a decision to refute them. We can be brave, when we are ready, and confront these ideas. Take one step at a time, and the reconstruction of truth begins. We can rebuke comments or media messages we hear that are unrealistic, unjust, and harmful. We can do this out loud in the moment of confrontation, or silently in our minds as we encounter them. We can recruit our own "board of directors"— people we trust (authors, for example, and helpful friends and family members) who can remind us of our worth and beauty, and the worth and beauty of others, when the world is working diligently to maintain the discriminative status quo.

Fourth, if dialogue is possible with groups or individuals who are making harmful statements, join with others and stand as an advocate to overtly challenge the destructive paradigms built into our society. You might initiate conversations, write about, or lobby for changes that would further secure respect for diversity and reinforce the value found in the uniqueness of all people.

These four approaches begin within the individual. It starts with each of us finding the power within to deconstruct negative systemic messaging and identify injustice. With these approaches, **we can reject oppression and dehumanization**. We can secure our right to self-acceptance, and we can move forward to usher in liberation and freedom. By using conflict as a catalyst for transformative work, we can create the space for the beginning of loving ourselves, and, concurrently, loving others, while reconstructing a more just and healthy paradigm in our society.

✳

watch your language: words matter

[CHAPTER NINE]

And by "Watch Your Language" I actually mean "We Sometimes Have Absolutely No Idea How Much Our Words Perpetuate Body Image Issues and Conversely How Much Changing Them Can Fix ALL the Problems," but that was too fucking long for a title, so I made a short one instead.

I'm surprised that you're even reading this after that bossy chapter title, but I'm glad you are. Because, ACTUALLY, this could be the most important chapter of all.

In my short time here on earth, and even shorter time preachin' body love, I've discovered there are certain times when words and how we use them are *really* important. Well, words are always important, but the body acceptance movement has brought attention to a few particular pockets of problematic conversation that we can improve on. Here are a few things to remember.

1. Beware of the "versus" monster.

Thanks to the setup of the beauty myth, it's become normal to compare, contrast, and compete with other women's bodies. Yes, even under the guise of *loving your body*. While I follow a good number of body-lovin' Facebook pages, I choose them very carefully. There are many pages run by those who are attempting to empower certain body types, but they do so by putting down another body type. The most classic example would be an image that says, "Bones are for the dogs, meat is for the man," or "Real women have curves." An especially offensive page adds to that tagline, "not the body of a 12-year-old boy." I've also seen "Fuck society. This [Marilyn Monroe] is more attractive than this [a bony Kate Bosworth]," and . . . well, good god, it's everywhere.

Internet, I think you're confused.

That is not really how body positivity works.

It goes the other way, too, and this thinking creates a monstrous "us versus them" dichotomy in the body acceptance world, which is what happens when thin women categorize fat women as lazy, and fat women pigeonhole thin women as "sellouts." None of this is constructive, and none of this is true. Here's a fact: We all deal with similar insecurities. As a fat woman, I am no stranger to detrimental comments regarding my weight. They may be well intentioned, or they may be pointedly cruel; regardless, they are all hurtful. But fat women are not the only ones who receive criticism about their weight; if we look at the opposite side of the spectrum we see the same patterns. "Skinny" people are also the target of encouraged bullying, bullying that is surprisingly similar to the kind that we fatties know all too well. I'm sure you've heard some of these:

1. "Eat a sandwich!"
2. "Must be nice to be so thin."
3. "Do you have an eating disorder?"

4. "You'd look so much better if you'd just put some meat on your bones."

5. "How can you be insecure when you're so small?"

6. "You're so skinny, I hate you."

7. "'Real' women have curves."

8. "Of course you're cold! You have no fat on you."

9. "I wish I had your problem."

Because there is such disdain toward larger bodies in our society, we've worked hard to counter that, and now we often associate the term "body positive" with embracing rolls, bellies, and arm flab. Now we've started filling the world with verbal and visual conversations about fat bodies and that, my friends, is kick-ass! We *must* counteract the negativity that we are fed daily and so I say: YES TO PRO-FAT! Yes yes yes! But let's not confuse pro-fat with anti-skinny. Let's not forget that our body positivity also applies to all shapes, sizes, sexes, shades, genders, abilities, and everything else our bodies are capable of being. The body love conversation needs to support *everyone*. Otherwise, what are we all fighting for?

In his book *Pedagogy of the Oppressed*, Paulo Freire talks about a phenomenon that happens often within oppressed groups: the development of sub-oppressors, or those within the demographic who are fighting for liberation but crushing others in order to do so. As Naomi Wolf points out, those who perpetuate the beauty myth have actually cultivated rivalry among women in order to create division.[1] Spurring competition among people is a classic distraction technique created to keep those who are oppressed busy fighting against each other instead of figuring out a way to get out from under their oppressors altogether. Our advertising culture LOVES that we do this; they gleefully continue to create their self-hate doctrine while we are distracted as we waste our energy pitting ourselves against our fellow strugglers when we could be using our energy to change the state of the world we live in. Let's NOT do ANY of that, okay? We all feel like we're flawed in some way because we are all comparing ourselves to the same ideal—and that ideal doesn't even exist. Never has. Never will. We must change the *system* together if we're ever gonna get outta this mess; we have to find equality all the way around. Comparison and competition don't serve anyone in the end.

> There is power in community, and there is power in numbers. If we support each other in our journeys, the sky is the limit.

In fact, celebrating each other's successes is kind of the answer.

Ever feel like someone else's win is your loss? Ain't true. I recently came across an amazing image on Instagram that reads, "Her success is not your failure," which I re-posted with the comment, "YES THIS." I'm happy to say this has been exactly my experience with every body advocate I've ever met. And this, dear friends, is a beautiful and rare thing in broader society.

I've watched teams and communities grow stronger and more successful when they bask in other's achievements. Celebrating someone else's success doesn't mean the others in the group fall behind, but rather that they all recognize the power of collective happiness. I believe this is true when it comes to loving our bodies as well.

The indescribably wonderful Virgie Tovar shared her mission in life with me once while we were sunbathing in San Jose, California: Her mission is to rid our society of its diet culture habits and *to help others be successful in doing the same.* Notice how she doesn't just aspire to kick ass at something; she also seeks to empower and hand off her knowledge to others. It was so refreshing to hear that, and this isn't an isolated incident. Magnificent activists like Sonya Renee, Marilyn Wann, and Lindsey Averill (and honestly almost every single activist I've ever come in contact with; it continues to blow my mind) have all gone out of their way to assist me in my endeavors. Because this is what it's all about—**this is how it's**

supposed to work. This is what the body love community stands for, and you're totally a part of that community.

It's a lovely thing, seeing people relish the successes of others. And I think the reason for this community's undying support of each other lies in the fact that every single one of us believes in empowerment. Positivity. Love.

I believe in body love. You believe in body love. And if we all really believe in body love, we'll want every person to find that as well. And once we *all* embrace that motherfucking love? OMG, MIRACLES will happen. There is power in community, and there is power in numbers. If we support each other in our journeys, the sky is the limit.

All body judgement is backward progression, and I say we ditch that. Let's ditch it altogether. Body positive is all inclusive. All bodies. All relevant.

2. Salad doesn't get you to heaven.

Not too long ago I was sitting outside at a creperie with my boyfriend, and as we were eating and chatting a woman sitting alone with her dog said out loud, to no one in particular but clearly directing her comment to us, "God, I'm glad my husband isn't here! He'd kill me if he knew I was breaking my diet and eating this food!"

She then sat in suspended silence waiting for us to answer. Maybe waiting for us to say, "Oh, *man*, you'd be in trouble!" or "Tsk, tsk, tsk!"

Instead we just resumed chatting and eating, and I'm sure I said something like "Jesus, these crepes are amazing," or something else positive about this food I was apparently supposed to be feeling guilt over.

My boy and I talked about the awkward situation later, and we decided that this woman's supposed diet wasn't the problem, necessarily (to each her own); it was the fact that she felt like she needed to hide her enjoyment of that food from her husband, and then make her apparent shame a casual topic of conversation with strangers . . . like it was a common thing to do.

Because it IS a common thing to do.

Women *bond* over diet talk. We love to share what we can and can't eat. We form connections over feeling guilty or superior about food. We smile sympathetically when someone says, "Oh, god, I was so *bad* and ate cheesecake last night!" or "I'm going to be *good* today and eat a salad."

DOES ANYONE ELSE THINK IT'S WEIRD THAT WE ASSIGN MORAL IMPLICATIONS TO FOOD? I didn't used to, but the more I thought about it the more I realized it's just fucking

> **You're not a better person if you eat carrots, and you're not a fuck-up if you eat pie.**

weird. Newsflash: Food isn't damnable. Food isn't virtuous. It's just delicious (most of it, anyway), so let's keep the conversation around it positive. Let me further clarify just in case we're not all on the same page: You're not a better person if you eat carrots, and you're not a fuck-up if you eat pie. That sustenance = salvation/damnation shit needs to stop already, y'feel?

So, what do you do if you personally stop demonizing and glorifying food, but your friends (or those strangers on the café patio) don't? I thought about how I wanted to respond next time a woman confesses her crepe sins to me, and I decided I would counter it with a sigh and a "That's so *BORING*." In fact, I've done this (several times, at work—I'm not sorry) and it works rather well. Some people find this rude and cruel and have suggested that perhaps I should try a softer (and more tactful) approach, and that's TOTALLY an option (and probably a better one), but if you really wanna shut that shit down, tell them it's boring and there are so many other things you can talk about. Like that awesome mail service where you can send your enemies envelopes full of glitter that gets all over everything and sticks around their house forever.

See. MUCH more interesting, yeah?

Redirect the conversation. Resume the enjoyment of your food. Revel in the fact that your spot in heaven isn't going to be determined by what's on your plate. Repeat.

3. Speak out if you feel forgotten.

There is a lot of criticism about who and what is included in (or rather, excluded from) the body positive movement . . . and rightfully so. As body love has surfaced into mainstream conversation, we've seen a tendency for the message to be delivered by and to straight, white, hourglass-shaped women (take ME, for example). Collectively we seem to cling to this spot and demographic, almost as if we are afraid to try anything more radical for fear the movement might lose its popularity. Which it might. But we should still try.

It's a tricky world to navigate, and introducing body positivity into a world immersed in decades of teaching that says otherwise is radical and impressive to be sure. But with this limited representation of bodies within the movement, there are those who are left out, further ostracized, and ignored. My education regarding bodies (other than the one I have lived in) has been gradual . . . but it's picking up speed daily. When I started in "activism," the first title of my lecture and the tagline for the Body Love Conference was "Change Your World. Not Your Body." The sentiment behind it had pure intentions: to illustrate how we can change our perspective and not feel the need to change our body in order to be okay. What I didn't realize back then was that this exhortation was most certainly exclusionary to those who felt like they DID need to change their bodies in order to fully be who they really were. This was brought up when I was in a meeting with several transgender faculty and community members, and I quickly saw the exclusion. That title is now "Change the World. Love Your Body."

I may be slow, but I'm working on it.

I was grateful for that particular group of gracious individuals for pointing out how important those words are. There is too much exclusion within the body positive community that happens out of ignorance (hi, me here), and it can usually be quickly changed if brought to the perpetrator's attention.

THE
FAT
PEOPLE:
do all the things!
CHALLENGE
✳

#8: JUMP IN AN ELEVATOR.

I would imagine that the ignorant people who say fat people shouldn't jump in elevators are concerned that this would break the hydraulic or rope system. Reality check: Most elevators can carry thousands of pounds. You are not going to jeopardize anyone's safety even if you were to jump six feet off the elevator floor. (If you do that, send me a video. I'd be so impressed.)

Your challenge: The jumping isn't the hard part. Taking a photo of it is. Try anyway.

For those who don't feel represented, you have all the permission in the world to use your words to change that. If you ever experience exclusivity in a movement that is trying to be inclusive, one of the most harmful things you can do is keep it to yourself. Discussing how fucked up something is can be helpful in finding solidarity and support, and ultimately it needs to be shared because others may not realize this form of exclusivity is even happening.

This book is a great example. I've done my best with my background and experiences to include as many issues and speak to as many people as possible. I will inevitably fail, however, at including everyone; maybe you are feeling this way. For that, I offer my apologies, and it would be really great if you could help me out. A perfect way to address this issue would be to email me a lovely note that says "Hey! It would be really beneficial if you could include _____ in the future!" Maybe even include a reason you feel this way.

Chances are, I'm gonna do just that. And I think that's true for a lot of activists, and even a lot of the world (clothing companies too—read on to see for yourself in the next chapter).

I get that it's frustrating and maddening, and that exclusivity affects our lives in a *monumental way*. But I can promise you something: If someone who's perpetuating exclusivity either doesn't realize it or only hears secondhand that someone (or a group of someones) is pissed about whateverithappenstobe, things may not change the way they should. On the other hand, an informative, politely worded (and maybe even kind!) email can make all the difference. Words have so much power, and when you consciously craft power in order to develop real change? SUPER power!

That's how we shift social consciousness, y'all . . . working WITH each other. Wait, am I repeating myself? That sounds oddly familiar.

4. Body commentary doesn't have to be a thing.

I'll never forget what Kim Kardashian looked like while she was pregnant. Why? *Because it was on the cover of every single tabloid magazine in every store ever.*

Another brilliantly evil component of our image-obsessed culture is that we have all been given (in the words of Virgie Tovar herself) a body police "deputy badge" by our body-hatin' world. I'm gonna ask you to turn that motherfucking badge *in*.

Here's why: Contrary to what we've been taught, other people's bodies are NOT ours to publicly comment on. Wait. What? I'll say it again: Other people's bodies are NOT ours to publicly comment on. Yeah, I know. Weird, right? Let that sink in.

It almost feels counterintuitive. We love to criticize *and* applaud other people's bodies; it's one of our primary forms of entertainment! From Jessica Simpson's weight gain to Jonah Hill's weight loss. From the cover showcasing Jennifer Garner's no-baby "baby bump" (which is often what happens when you have several kids, and, in fact, at the time of publication of this book she was not expecting) to the spreads of the forty hottest celebrities alive. From Taylor Swift's belly button (gasp! She has one!) to Amanda Palmer's nipple. From the person on the street looking "great" in the leather leggings to the person wearing the "terrible" SpongeBob unitard in Walmart . . . we're obsessed.

But to think we have the right to comment on someone else's appearance is a false assumption. First of all: Negative comments about another person's body? Nuh-uh. Never. No place. No how. Period. That's easy.

But wait, what about positive comments? Well, it depends on whom you ask. Some people like 'em; some people don't like any comments about their bodies. But if you're giving someone a nice word, be aware of what you're sayin'. I betcha dol-

> **Contrary to what we've been taught, other people's bodies are NOT ours to publicly comment on.**

lars to pink-sprinkled donuts that half of the "compliments" given aren't actually very nice at all. Oh, I know. It's tricky. There are several good articles on what NOT to tell your friend who's lost weight, and I think it's a great example of how to avoid "negatively complimenting" someone. Yes, negatively complimenting someone is a thing.

Take for example, the comment, "You look so good, I didn't recognize you!" The person is insinuating (not subtly) that you're unrecognizable as "you," and before you were unsightly and now you are not. This is NOT a compliment. Then there's a comment like, "Wow, you look good, but I liked the way you looked before." This may be an attempt at a more supportive angle, but it still discredits the body you have now. This is also NOT a compliment.

This might seem hypersensitive and therefore confusing or annoying, and might make some say "WELL GOD, then I won't say ANYTHING about how they look!" To which I would say: Maybe that's a good idea.

We have a lot more to talk about than our bodies, for the record. Like the fact that my cat got a bloody nose when I was trying to "kidnap" him to take him to the vet, and how horrifying that was. OR, that Jesus GOD it's eighty degrees in Tucson and it's only *February*. Or, wow, I just took two weeks off from Facebook and it was the best vacation I've ever had! Or, yeah, LET'S talk about Obamacare and how it impacts the people and paychecks.

Oh wait.

That's just me?

Well, you can choose to talk about whatever you want (my cat's nose is *fine*, btw), but the POINT is, that there are a LOT of other things to talk about besides someone's appearance. And more often than not, appearance is a triggering subject that often leaves the subject of your commentary with an unhelpful internal dialogue that lasts much longer than the actual conversation. So, when in doubt? Talk about something else, *especially* when addressing strangers.

But what if you WANT to compliment someone (assuming it's a friend or family member) on how they look, and you know the person would appreciate it? That's cool. Lots of people like to hear that they're lookin' fine. Just be careful how you say it. Blogger Bevin Branlandingham nails it here: "I like to create an environment in my life that is about substance over small talk, where compliments are genuine and weight is value-neutral."[2]

Mm-hmm. That.

Weight is one of the most loaded subjects (hence the fact that this book exists), so if you want to compliment someone, ladies, I'd suggest complimenting something other than their body size. "That outfit is sexy as fuck," or "Your hair is amazing" are compliments that don't minimize or magnify body issues and commentary. You can even go for the non-appearance compliment and say "God, you're brilliant tonight," or "You're so radiantly YOU tonight . . . I absolutely love it."

You catch my drift? I mean, don't get me wrong. I'm not saying you should keep all your kind thoughts to yourself! I'll tell friends that they look fucking great all the time. Great can mean a million things; the important thing is to mean what you say and not pigeonhole the conversation by specifically referring to weight (gained *or* lost), which could be perceived as judgmental. 'Cause that's just a black hole none of us wanna get stuck in.

What if your friend *brings up* her weight or the fact that she's lost it? Bevin says that if people talk about their weight in a positive manner, a good way to contribute would be to say, "I think you look great at any weight, but I'm really glad you feel good in your body right now." If they're negative, try, "I think you look great regardless of what size you are. And I mean it," and move on to another subject.[3]

Too complicated? Pissed that I'm even talking about it? Well, to keep it simple, if your compliment is genuine, kind, and directed to a person you know . . . there's a good chance it's gonna be okay.

But hold on, what about when others comment on our weight/ appearance and it's NEGATIVE? What words do we use then?

This, my friend, is an EXCELLENT question, and it all depends on your comfort level. I present to you three options for confronting people who just don't get it and think they have a right to criticize your body.

THE MILITANT AND IN-YOUR-FACE APPROACH

Tired of people saying shitty things and not being called out on it? This one's for you.

Virgie Tovar shared the following story about her personal fat-shaming tactics in *Hot & Heavy: Fierce Fat Girls on Life, Love & Fashion*. On the train in San Francisco, a clearly misguided woman whispered loudly to her partner that Virgie was too fat to be wearing whatever outfit she had on. Knowing Virgie, it was probably something unapologetic and skintight with a cheetah print and a rockin' necklace you couldn't ignore if you tried.

That girl? Well, she didn't take it sitting down. Virgie walked over, stood face-to-face with the woman, and explained that her body was her own, that she's free to wear what she wants, that there was no reason for the woman to feel intimidated by her outfit, and that she looked *great*, and knew it.

Note the lack of insults or criticism of the woman or her appearance. "I simply felt it polite to inform her that the era of fat-girl apologies and tastelessly retrograde fatphobic remarks is coming to a close and the day of the fierce, too-much-to-handle fat girl is close at hand."[4]

And that is how you shut that shit down.

THE SASSY-UNDERPANTS APPROACH

Feeling a little bit fiery, but don't want to get up in anyone's grill about it? I have the perfect solution. It's directly from Ragen Chastain from the blog *Dances with Fat*, and it's a pretty damn decent guideline if you ask me. So decent, in fact, that if it became implemented in a worldwide way, it would, in her words "end about 90% of the jackassery and fuckwittery that happens on the internet, and maybe 50% that happens in the real world." So consider your utilization of this rule a gift to humanity.

Here's how it goes: "The Underpants Rule," Ragen explains, just means "everyone is the boss of their own underpants." Meaning, you're a big kid wearing big-kid underpants, and thus you are capable of living your own life according to your own rules, thankyouverymuch. So, according to Ragen, "it's not your job to tell other people what to do and it's not their job to tell you what to do." Pretty simple.

Based on that, then, she continues:

If someone is considering saying something that starts with

- *People should*
- *Everyone ought to*
- *What people need to do*
- *We should all*
- *Nobody should*
- *You shouldn't*
- *blah blah things that have to do with underpants that aren't yours blah blah*

then there is a 99.9% chance that they are about to break The Underpants Rule.[5]

Genius, amiright? Dear god, imagine if everyone followed that rule . . .

. . .

. . .

. . .

Whoops, I'm back. I got lost in Body Autonomy Utopia for a sec there.

ANYWAY, this rule: How do you use it? When someone makes a comment about your appearance that you don't appreciate, you simply say, "Excuse me, but I'm a grown-ass adult and I am in charge of my own underpants. If I wanted you all up IN my underpants, you would have been the first to know. Since I haven't invited you, I would appreciate it if you would leave me, my body, and my very-much-only-mine underpinnings alone, and I'll be happy to do the same for you," or something along those lines.

Of course, saying "you should use The Underpants Rule" is in fact breaking The Underpants Rule itself, so I'll just leave it to you to decide if it's the right approach for you.

But if you do use it and it doesn't quiet someone's rude commentary, I dunno what will.

THE SIMPLE SELF-ADVOCACY APPROACH

This might be a good approach to start out with. When someone says something negative about you, your appearance, or your body, simply state: "I would really appreciate it if you would keep your comments about my body to yourself."

If it's a family member or close friend, maybe even, "It really hurts me when you make negative comments about my body. I would prefer that you refrain from doing so." Or whatever version of that in your own words feels comfortable. Practice it so it feels normal and so that, even when you feel like freezing up, the words are ready to be said. I believe in you.

Not feeling up to ANY of those? Try this line: "Well, that's *one* opinion." It's my favorite.

***

The thing to take away from all of this, besides the actual words, is that you're totally able to stand up for yourself. It's not weird, inappropriate, or uncalled for to say these things. Gone are the days of sitting in shame, hiding your face, or running away. From here on out you get to call the shots.

Because: *Your* underpants, remember?

And whatever you end up doing, just remember that no matter what you choose or what they say, you're totally okay just the way you are, and they are the ones who need to check the abominable behavior, like something fierce. Making negative comments about your or anyone's body to your face (or to your back) isn't okay, it's a dick move.

I suppose the last option would be to silently walk away from such people and never talk to them again. This would also work. Your call. When all is said and done, their bullshit is not your bullshit. So don't take it on. Just keep on bein' your rockin' self, okay?

5. Be conscious of appropriate terminology to the best of your ability.

There are a lot of politically correct ways to address overlooked groups of people, and it's a really wonderful thing to educate yourself on how to do so appropriately.

For some it might seem like an inconvenience, but really all I'm asking of you is to work a titch harder; by doing so, you'll be eliminating a little of the harm that is so often directed at others. You'll have to learn a couple of new words, but you'll also be assisting in the reframing of harmful vocabulary used against others. Less pain in the world just by switching vocabulary? Totally worth it.

A simple example is: If you're unsure which gender pronoun to use when addressing someone, the best way to find out is simply to ask.

That easy. Doesn't perpetuate a world of hurt, it educates you, and it supports the person.

Try to also be cognizant of words that are only used within subgroups, such as "crip," "trans," and even "fat." Just like I, along with many other fat people, am reclaiming the word fat (though without knowing a person's preference, it might not be appropriate for others to use it when addressing larger bodies), other groups might also be finding power in choosing words that become their own, but when someone who is not a part of the group (who doesn't fully understand the issues at hand) uses it, that can trigger the negative connotations still associated with the word in our society.

Over the last year, my body activism has drastically changed to become far more diverse and inclusive, and while it's far from perfect, this change has come as a result of people sharing their suggestions with me (see above, "3. Speak out if you feel forgotten"). Thanks to this newfound consciousness, I started asking a lot of questions. It's been a slow process, but I'm working on it.

I'm still learning, and am still, at times, somewhat terrified of accidentally offending someone. But then I tell myself (and others): If you make a mistake, don't freak out. You can't know what you don't know, but now you do; so, put the new knowledge in your pocket and use it next time. It's an imperfect process, but making a genuine attempt at dissolving existing discrimination can go a long way.

6. Deflecting awesomeness is for suckers.

I grew up thinking that modesty and humility were some of the most virtuous traits a person (read: woman) could have. NOT ANYMORE.

Obviously, we don't want to trample others in the quest toward self-esteem, but there are so many missed opportunities to verbally hug ourselves. For example, the next time someone genuinely compliments you, try accepting the kind words and say, "Thank you!" instead of "Oh god, really? I feel terrible today!"

We're taught to deflect compliments, to publicly berate ourselves, and that verbal flogging is a sign of a good human being. It's not. Having the nerve to say, "God, I'm feeling so wonderful about myself today!" is a fantastic thing, and if it makes people uncomfortable (it might) it's because they haven't figured out that form of liberation yet. Their loss.

Some might not agree with my assertive opinion on this, but I believe that modesty and humility are tools used to keep people in line. Get out of that fucking line and love yourself like you deserve to be loved, already. Okay?

7. When it comes to kids, they're kinda like parrots.

Many of the "I need advice!" emails I receive are along the lines of: "How can I teach my kid to be more body positive?" Well, I don't have kids, but I've had some amazing conversations with those that do, and, y'know . . . watched some online videos.

But don't worry. I'm not going to sit here and give you parenting tips that I got from YouTube videos.

What I will share with you is from an incredibly adorable video that went viral a few years ago called "Jessica's Daily Affirmation" (watch it), in which a four-year-old stands on top of a sink, looks in the mirror, power punches while dancing, and yells the greatest gratitude list I've ever heard, including things she was grateful for: her parents, her home, her hair, and that she was good at *all* the things.[6]

Then she hops off the sink and runs down the hallway singing. Yes, I find this four-year-old inspiring, and yes, I'm thinking I need to make a list of affirmations like this to sing every day. Forever. Affirmations are a wonderful tool to give to both adults and children (and if you want more ideas, Chapter 11 was created JUST for that!). I'd recommend trying to facilitate a conversation about (or making a list of) affirmations that might work for your little ones. Perhaps even role modeling by creating and doing your own would be beneficial for both of you.

Another thing parents can do with their kids is normalize other body shapes and appearances. Children most likely won't be getting this from the outside world. If your child asks you a question like, "Why is that man wearing a wig?" you have the chance to say something neutral—or, even better, positive—that directs your child toward accepting things that look "different" from what they see on television or what is presented as standard in their outside world.

Other tips and tricks from the magic body love kit: Stay away from calling "fat" a feeling ("I feel so fat!") and always connecting skinny with healthy. You can teach your kids the correct definition of "healthy," which has nothing to do with body size! Compliment little girls on things other than saying, "You look so pretty!" Look through magazines and have discussions about altered photos, and talk about what Photoshop is and *why* it's used. Teach kids that bodies come in all shapes and sizes. Be aware of when your kids are bullied and how it's handled. When we teach kids to "ignore" bullies, we are also teaching them that the bullies have power; that they might be right. Arm your kid with words to use in the situation and the words to use when telling an adult what is happening. I wish more kids were encouraged to report bullying instead of just allowing it to happen. I'm going to teach my kids to SNITCH LIKE HELL.

Emphasize the cool, amazing, and incredible things that our bodies can do that have nothing to do with what they look like! THAT one I think I love the most. OUR BODIES ARE SO FUCKING AWESOME AND DO AMAZING THINGS, GUYS! Like heal wounds. And grow hair. Our skin rejuvenates itself and is water resistant. And our bodies breathe on their own. And digest food on the inside without any help. Of course, not all bodies can do every one of those things, but all bodies do their own versions of amazing things, so let's find 'em and celebrate them! I wish that we as adults would talk about that more, too.

Martin Luther King Jr. was convinced that children are the

solution to change, and that if they grow up learning equality, love, and the importance of diversity, then we'll all live in a better world sooner than we think. I tend to agree. So thank you moms, dads, and others raising kiddos, for working to instill empowering, inclusive concepts in our little ones. So much of our body hate is learned from those who raise us, and I'm glad to hear there are so many of you looking to redirect that thinking. You're pretty kick-ass.

Yeah.

Because I'm great at teaching adults rather than kids, I found someone who was. Or, rather, two someones: Teachers Lauren Pinto and Meagan Kimm, who have developed seminars in Burbank, California, to help school-aged kids build self-esteem, have a body positive outlook, and reach a level of self-discovery. I asked Laura and Meagan what *they* would tell parents who are trying to help their children's body love bloom. Drawing on their combined years in the classroom, Laura and Meagan have compiled a list just for YOU!

LAUREN AND MEAGAN'S FIVE TIPS FOR RAISING KICK-ASS, BODY POSITIVE KIDS

1. **Model, model, model:** Modeling in the classroom is when teachers provide a quality example of what they're teaching. For you, a parent or caregiver, modeling means you are the example your child will base their behaviors, attitudes, values, and lifestyle on. This means any comment you make about yourself ("Do these jeans make me look fat?") or the comments you make about others ("She should not be wearing that!") are all heard and internalized by your child. In order to infuse their lives with body positivity, you have to make sure that what you're modeling and what you're saying to them are in sync with your values.

2. **Develop the whole child:** Our society has the tendency to put a lot of value on the way we look. Since you're reading this book,

you know how overwhelming this is, so imagine how intense that can be for your child. It's important your child see you put value into a variety of different areas outside of the way you look. Now, for a parent, that's not to say you have to enroll your child in an art class, sign them up for peewee football, get them the best acting coach, and buy fifteen different pairs of dance shoes. Instead, you can expose them to a variety of life experiences in small, yet significant ways.

The chart below includes examples for the different areas that could start a conversation between you and your child and expose them to a new appreciation of the world around them.

AREAS	PROMPTS
Academics	At the dinner table: "How do you feel about your math test"?
	In the car ride home: "What cool thing did you learn in English class?
Arts	Driving down the freeway: "I really like that mural. What do you think?"
	Listening to the radio: "That song is so catchy! My favorite part is. . . . What's yours?"
Community	Look for ways to volunteer your time: raking the neighbor's yard, picking up trash you see, offering to open a door for someone, holding the elevator, sharing your food at lunch
Sports	"How about them New York Giants?"
	"They trained really hard for that game."
	"How long do you think they had to practice that play to get it right?"

(continues)

Health	Reminding them of all the amazing things their bodies can do (other than the way they look): "That scar on your knee is healing. Isn't it cool that your body can repair itself like that?"

We as people are not solely how we look. Each person has unique interests, talents, and thoughts. When we as adults embrace the diversity within ourselves and encourage it in our children, we can appreciate and learn from everyone around us.

3. **Meet them where they're at**: In our experiences, this is the area with the hardest buy-in. That is because it requires honest conversation about topics like sex, bullying, death, friendship troubles, divorce and the other depressing life woes, all in a language children can understand. This is difficult because these are not easy topics for you or your child to talk about, let alone with each other. The best way to ease into these types of conversations is to take the initiative and notice cues from your child such as when they come home from school upset, do things outside their usual routine, or are asking about something above their age level.

   Now you might be wondering what this has to do with body positivity. We've learned from our students that concern over their looks becomes an issue at a young age. We've worked with first graders who are scared to be fat, and others who are already using it as an insult. Coupled with the amount of media children are exposed to, as well as our society's obsession with flawless appearance, it's easy to understand why poor body image is becoming such a problem. As your child grows more mature, your conversations will too.

4. **Remember that it's a process:** In order for your child to have a body positive outlook, you need to have one, too. In writing,

that seems so simple but it's important to remember that this is a process and it's not going to happen overnight! It's going to take time to understand what you find important, change your outlook, and find ways to model this for your child. But practice makes progress; the more you are trying to interject body positivity in your life, the more body positivity will manifest.

5. **End on a positive:** As I'm sure you know, it's easy to get wrapped up in the bad: what should have happened, what could have been said, what didn't go according to plan. But taking an active stance on finding the good that came from a hectic day or terrible situation can reframe the experience. Focusing on the positive turns the situation into a growth experience, and allows you to reflect on it in a balanced way.

And, I'll add, go easy on yourself while you're attempting to teach a young human something that we're all still learning. That goes for teaching yourself as well. I've always been taught that practice makes progress . . . not perfect. And I hold onto that concept always.

That goes for the rest of the traps and tips as well. We're all so conditioned to bond over something "evil"—like *gasp* cake—and comment on each other's appearances that WE'RE GONNA SLIP UP ONCE IN A WHILE. Don't sweat it. If you need to, send a "Sorry 'bout that" someone's way, and cut yourself a break. Do better next time and remember that practice makes progress, especially when you're a human. Which I'm betting you are.

MY TRANS MASCULINITY HAS CURVES, FAT, AND ATTITUDE

SAM DYLAN FINCH OF LET'S QUEER THINGS UP

I am a genderqueer kid who presents in a masculine sort of way. I'm not a man, not a woman, and happily rocking something in between.

My journey began with a gut feeling: It was like femininity was a tight, tiny space that I tried, helplessly, to squeeze myself into. "Girl" was a box that always felt too small. And as I got older, I felt a strong disconnect from the label "woman," like it was something I was told about myself but never quite believed. What began as a gut feeling evolved into an ever-present anxiety that I couldn't shake, a splinter under the surface that I couldn't find but knew was there.

It wasn't until I was a college undergrad at the ripe age of seventeen, studying gender and sexuality, that I finally began to uncover a whole new vocabulary. Words like "genderqueer" and "androgyny," which allowed me to discard "woman" and instead express my gender in my own unique way. Words like "transgender" and "transmasculine," which gave me the chance to abandon my assigned gender and adopt a new kind of masculinity instead of the femininity that had previously felt so inescapable. All these words began to orbit me in a fantastic blur, novel and important and exciting. At the center of this new language, I began to put together the puzzle that had eluded me for so long: my own gender.

I realized I had a choice. So I gave myself permission to express myself in masculine and androgynous ways, piecing together an image of me that felt more honest than ever before. Androgyny and masculinity were no longer off-limits, and it was freeing at first. That is, until I collided with the expectations of everyone around me.

When I call myself androgynous, folks have a very certain image in mind: thin, flat, lacking curves. Androgyny has its own norms, as any Google search will tell you (seriously—search "androgyny" and be amazed/appalled). Imagine the surprise when I show up to give a talk, and an adorably chunky, curvy queer walks up to the podium. Androgyny has become synonymous with stick-thin, straight up and down, which meant my chubby and curvy body was not welcome in *that* club. There are chiseled jaws and hollow cheekbones as far as the eye can see, well-defined facial features with high contrast, something my round and filled-out face would never in a million years resemble.

I've felt pressured to fit into that mold of "androgyny": the idea that, to be gender neutral, I have to literally shape-shift or somehow contort my body into an entirely new shape. And let me tell you, that ain't happenin'. Bind as I may, layer as I might, these curves aren't going anywhere.

This used to distress me. I used to feel less valid as a trans person because my body did not fit the ideal. It's funny how, even in genderqueer and non-binary communities, we're slowly but surely creating body norms and expectations that are just as constricting as the ones we left behind when we transitioned.

It wasn't just about being thin anymore; it was about hiding my shape, flattening my chest into oblivion, tailoring my clothes to balance out my body, and hoping I would be forgiven for taking up space.

Sometimes I didn't know if I wanted that body because it would make me feel more like myself, or if I craved that body because this is what androgynous people were "supposed" to look like. If queer liberation was about being our authentic selves, how had authenticity become so muddled with all these impossible ideals? I didn't want to hide my body. The emotional impact of being told, again and again, that your validity depends on how well you can mask your body felt wrong. The idea that I had to conform to a certain body type to be valid in my gender was problematic, and in connecting with others in my community, I quickly found that I wasn't the only one who felt this pressure.

I began writing articles at my blog, *Let's Queer Things Up!*, confessing the invalidation I often felt as a curvy androgynous person. Almost immediately, I was flooded with emails from other androgynous and transmasculine people, folks who said, "I'm fat, and I'm curvy, and I'm queer, but everywhere I turn, I'm told that bodies like mine aren't androgynous." A transmasculine friend of mine confessed that they couldn't bring themselves to come out as transgender, because they were afraid no one would believe them. They said to me, "Sam, unless I find a binder that can turn a pear into a rectangle, no one will see me the way I see myself. I'm queer, but no one will believe me."

My community of androgynous queers, folks who just wanted to be authentically themselves, were coming up against an impossible norm that told them their bodies were somehow not enough—that androgyny was reserved for a certain body type, and if you were some other way, you were shit out of luck.

Androgyny was supposed to be about diverse-gender expressions and, consequently, diverse bodies. But instead it was a whitewashed, fat-erasing, curve-hating body ideal that almost no one could live up to. Women and men weren't the only ones who needed body positivism; my community of genderqueer and androgynous folks needed a good helping of self-love, too.

So instead of hiding myself underneath layers upon layers or wearing a size-too-small binder that made my ribs ache, I stopped punishing my body and myself and started looking for ways to create a loving relationship with myself. No doubt, the dysphoria was still real—there were times I couldn't leave my apartment for days because my chest made me feel like my head had been placed on the wrong body. But there is a difference between my dysphoria and society's discomfort with my body; there is a difference between my own dysphoria and society's disbelief that I can exist as I am.

Part of my journey in self-love was getting to a place where I could believe that my fat and my curves did not invalidate my gender identity or my masculinity.

It was affirming, in community and in reflection, to understand that my body was not the failure here. It was society's failure to recognize that gender (or the lack thereof) comes in all shapes and all sizes. This very narrow and specific idea of androgyny as a single shape and size leaves many genderqueer folks feeling invalid and forces them back into the closet before they've had the chance to live outside of it.

And I say: Fuck that.

I've got fat, I've got curves, and there's no need to hide it. I am 100 percent trans, 100 percent queer, and there's not a single beauty standard in the world that can tell me otherwise.

Someday I may get top surgery. Someday I may start hormone therapy. But I won't be doing it on someone else's terms. I won't modify my body for someone else's consumption or comfort. The changes I make to my body will be for me, and only me—because of my own discomfort and not the discomfort or disbelief of others.

I refuse to modify my body only because society refuses to recognize my gender unless I am a particular size and shape. And I refuse to hide my curves or my body just to fit into a narrow ideal of what it means to be "androgynous."

The validity of our gender identities does not depend on our size. There's nothing that we need to do to be valid. We were enough today, we will be enough tomorrow, and we will be enough always. Because there are no rules that say gender has to be performed or worn a particular way—we invent the rules.

And I say that my masculinity can be fat, curvy, and full of attitude. To hell with anyone who says otherwise.

✳

"fatshion" is a form of political resistance: wear what scares you

[CHAPTER TEN]

"There's an adrenaline rush that comes with denying the common rules of society: that I should always be trying to lose weight, that I should always be unhappy with some flaw. To say I am perfectly content with my body and all the parts that assemble it is nothing less than radical."

—*Virgie Tovar*

Did you know that wearing a dress with horizontal stripes is the same as holding a sign that says Fuck the Man?

Well, it kinda is.

When I started out as a body love and advocacy blogger, I purposefully stayed far away from "fatshion" (fat + fashion) posts for years. I felt like my talking about potent political subjects instead of peplum skirts would be a *far* better use of readers' time. But I was kinda wrong.

As I explored the world of body advocacy and started to embrace my unconventional shape, this eventually (years later, mind you) led to me to an outright refusal to follow societal rules of what I could and could not do.

And with this rebellion and interspersed fashion defiance, I realized something. Fashion rules are for people who don't know that they're breakable . . . and I wasn't going to be that person any longer.

You know the fashion rules I'm talking about. We've all heard the plus-size rule about avoiding horizontal stripes. About wearing black because it's slimming. About wearing flared pants instead of tapered so we look "proportional." About avoiding small patterns so we don't look like furniture. Don't wear *giant* print because you'll overwhelm the viewer. Don't wear halters. Don't wear sleeveless. Don't wear chunky jewelry. Don't wear texture. Don't wear shiny fabric. Don't wear spandex. Don't wear baggy clothes. Don't. Don't. Don't. Don't.

But "LOVE yourself," the world still somehow tries to say, "by playing to your *strengths* and hiding your *flaws!*"

Two years ago, I finally said *no fucking more, y'all*. I had been bending over backwards to follow these ubiquitous guidelines, and because of this the list of things I wore but hated was miles long. And the list of things I didn't wear but loved was even longer still.

It was only by ignoring the rules and wearing what I wanted that I started to realize fashion was political. That the concept of not trying to minimize or hide your body was controversial. **That the act of publicly loving your body, allowing it to take up space, and dressing it up in whatever you liked . . . is revolutionary.** And this applies to all bodies, no matter their size, shape, shade, or age. When you love yourself, it blows people's minds.

I discovered the power behind choosing things I longed to wear but in the past hadn't allowed myself to. Because it would accentuate my underarms. Because it would show too much thigh. Because someone would be able to see my scandalous cleavage. Because it's too loud. Because it's too masculine. Because it's a drop waist. Because it's ugly. Because it's tight. Because it's loose. Because it's metallic. **Because of all the wrong reasons.**

And *that's* why I started a series of posts called "I Wear What I Want."

"I Wear What I Want" became my monthly outfit proclamations. Visual proof that any body could rock any look. I started documenting the smashing of personal style rules: strappy sandals, crop tops, sleeveless dresses, vinyl miniskirts, swimsuits, not-exactly business casual, maxi-skirts, AND short hair. It's been beyond liberating.

They may seem silly to some, but each was a huge deal for me. The short hair especially.

Ever seen something like this on the web when talking about short hairstyles?

> *When choosing a hairstyle that suits you, be sure to keep your weight in mind. If you have feminine features, you can choose a short haircut like a pixie cut that will bring your beauty to the viewers attention and will distract them from your weight. Otherwise, a longer cut may be more flattering.*

Of course you have. The idea that "overweight" ladies probably shouldn't have a short crop is ubiquitous and the words "conceal," "hide," and "distract from" are just as common. I bought into this for the majority of my life, and I never cut it shorter than an inch below my jawline. Fuck body shame, man. That stuff is poison.

When I was a teenager I was obsessed with the TV talk show *Regis and Kelly*. I would watch it religiously every morning, in love with the fake window and fake view of New York City and terribly awkward banter. God, I loved them. I will never forget the episode when Kelly was pregnant and talked about how she would never cut her hair super short because she felt like bigger hair distracted from her growing body.

Yep. Been there. Only not pregnant. YaknowwhatImean?

Here is the thing: The whole concept is kind of ridiculous. If you're fat, you're going to be fat no matter the length of your hair. People didn't think I was thin on Tuesday and then see me on Thursday and realize I was fat; no one fainted out of shock. It doesn't work that

THE
**FAT
PEOPLE:**
do all the things!
CHALLENGE
✳

#9: WEAR IRONIC SHIRTS.

After seeing t-shirts sold for soon-to-be-moms saying: "I'm not fat. Just pregnant." I knew I needed my own version.

So I made one: "I'm not pregnant. Just fat."

Hell yeah, I have a burrito bump! Tucson is the most delicious burrito capital of the United States and that may *sound* like my opinion, but there is a chance that it's also the truth. No shame in my game; I love burritos more than I love anyone else's opinion of my body.

I wore that kick-ass shirt all day while I ran errands around town. I felt like a sexy bitch, and the reactions were overwhelmingly positive whether I was at the market, a schmancy restaurant, or the alternative bookstore. More compliments and smiles than usual. I also got lots of discounts. That was reason enough to wear the shirt.

Your challenge: Make or find a shirt that YOU love. Something ironic. Something sarcastic. Something funny. A shirt with a middle finger . . . whatever you want.

way. Hair is not a magic cloak. Clothing is not a magic cloak. It's an expression of what you love, and I love short hair and tight clothing. AND I'LL WEAR WHAT I WANT, GODDAMNIT.

To say "Wear whatever you want" is empowering, but it hasn't always been easy to achieve. Any Generation X fat girl knows what it's like to have to shop in the men's section, chop off sleeves, get rid of the choking neckline, and try to make something you like out of . . . well, not much.

And while we have more options than a few decades ago, we've still got a long way to go.

A perfect example is the plus-size line Target launched called Ava & Viv.

The backstory: A little while ago, Target (the affordable favorite of trendy girls, and my *other* therapy office) launched a kick-ass collection: Altuzarra for Target. The chic clothing was gilded, cinched, and . . . outrageously wonderful. And none of them in plus sizes. Like, zero options for the larger lady.

A favorite gal and blogger of mine, Chastity of the blog *GarnerStyle*, wrote an open letter (an *effective tactic*, to be reinforced later) to the store, declaring a boycott because of the blatant exclusion. It went like this:

> *Dear Target,*
>
> *For so long, I loved you. I always went above and beyond in our relationship. I'll visit you to get a couple of items and more than a couple hundred dollars later and a cart full of products, I have left giving you way more than I ever planned to. No matter how much I give, you never seem to appreciate me. All I want is the clothing you offer all your other regular sized customers, but you always leave me out. With that being said, I have to end this relationship. It's you, not me and for my own well-being and my self-dignity I have to sever ties between us.*
>
> *This may seem a little dramatic, but the recent release of the photos of* **Altuzarra for Target** *collection has me feeling slighted. I'm up late, working as usual, and I see* **Refinery 29** *post 50 photos of the newest designer collaboration. Literally 50 pieces of beautiful (and I mean beautiful) affordable clothing and none of it will be remotely close to the size that I wear. The collection consists of deeps hues of burgundy, fabulous snakeskin prints, and fall worthy silk-like maxi dresses . . . enough to make any fashion lover lust. My heart sinks. You have once again made me feel like a second-class*

customer and because of that I'm going to have to discontinue
my relationship with you altogether.

  Year after year, season after season, you put out these
gorgeous designer collections and you almost never include a
plus range. Every time each of these collections is about to be
released it feels like a slap in the face. To add insult to injury,
over 6 months ago, you took most of your plus size clothing out
of the store, promising me something new and improved and
that has yet to happen. I've been in this abusive relationship
with you for far too long. I can't do this anymore. I will be
personally boycotting Target altogether. No more housewares,
grocery shopping, electronics . . . nothing. I'm done.

  You may ask, "Is there any way I will take you back?" I will
take you back, when and only when, you include true plus
sizes in your designer range collaborations. Until then, I will
take my money elsewhere.

Your Scorned Lover,
Chastity of GarnerStyle[1]

It caught on like wildfire on Twitter, and before you knew it . . .
there was a nationwide evacuation from the store.

Kinda.

Plus ladies were PISSED (and honestly, after a history that includes
removing fat girl clothing from stores, mislabeling pregnant clothing
as plus-size, and naming the colors of plus dresses things like "mana-
tee gray" while the straight sizes were called "dark heather gray"—yes,
really—I feel like it's only fair to be pissed), and so Target paid attention
to the recent online outrage . . . thank fucking GOD.

Refinery29 reported that Joshua Thomas, a spokesperson for
Target, then responded with something like: We never want to make
our customers sad, so we're sorry, will listen, and are launching a new
plus line soon.[2]

They then collaborated with three bloggers (who served as consultants for the line) and launched Ava & Viv, a new exclusive plus-size line only from Target. Guess what was in it? Gilding? Snake skin? Cinching?

NOPE.

Basics. T-shirts. Denim. TUNICS. Fucking tunics.

Okay, but hold on. BEFORE you get too angry, let me tell you something: This is progress. It may not seem like it, but the misguided line leaves me hopeful, and there are two reasons why:

1. The models they used for the "lookbook" were fat girls. Like, fat FAT girls . . . not padded, standard agency, size-8 models. Using Chastity, Gabi Gregg, and Nicolette Mason, they included body shapes and sizes that *we do not* see in plus fashion. This is an exceptional moment for so many plus bodies that never feel represented.

2. They were forced to listen to the outrage. I'll be the first to tell you the Internet is as horrific as it is helpful, but in this case, it had the power to give voice to the thousands of women who needed to be heard. And that's a beautiful thing. Because of the ruckus created online, a giant corporation (one that has almost two thousand locations in the U.S.) was more or less arm-wrestled into providing *something* for a very underserved group of women.

Are the pieces dated? Yes. Is the selection limited? Yep. Is it enough? Not even close. But is it a start? Oh, hell yeah.

I'm so encouraged by the shift in consumer consciousness that we're seeing nowadays. We've got a long way to go, but we are speaking up and being heard more than ever before. And it can be *really* influential.

Another great example of the power of the people can be found in the "tragic" story of Abercrombie & Fitch. I love this particular story, not only because it's a drastic example of a giant group of people saying "no" to the status quo, but also because it gave me the chance to get almost naked and have my pictures taken.

I like just about anything that gives me a chance to get almost naked and have my pictures taken.

If you missed the news coverage, in March 2013, some comments Abercrombie & Fitch CEO Mike Jeffries had made in 2006 resurfaced and caused . . . well, let's just say worldwide outrage.

Jeffries's declaration about the Abercrombie & Fitch target market was shared online over and over: "Candidly, we go after the cool kids. We go after the attractive all-American kid with a great attitude and a lot of friends. A lot of people don't belong [in our clothes], and they can't belong. Are we exclusionary? Absolutely."³ This statement, combined with the irrefutable sizeism of the company's refusal to offer women's clothing in size extra-large, brought big attention to A&F, and became a repeated news headline.

Where before A&F could get away with its elitist marketing and advertising practices, Matthew Shaer writes in *New York* Magazine, consumers have gradually stopped buying it:

> [Previously] consumers seemed to accept that Abercrombie's gleefully offensive vibe was part of the package, and the company's bottom line was never truly threatened.
> But sensibilities have since evolved; casual prejudice is not as readily tolerated. Today's teens are no longer interested in "the elite, cool-kid thing" to the extent that they once were, says [University of Michigan business school assistant professor Erik] Gordon. . . . "This generation is about inclusiveness and valuing diversity. It's about not looking down on people." And with the help of social media, for the first time critics have succeeded in putting Abercrombie on the defensive.⁴

For me, a person who faces weight discrimination on the daily, Jeffries's comments went in one ear and right out the other. That was, until I was asked SO MANY TIMES by readers posting on my Facebook page to address the issue . . . that I finally did.

The concept that fat women aren't attractive or worthy of inclusion was what needed to be addressed, and it seemed only appropriate to challenge that assumption using the style of the brand's overtly sexual advertisements. I teamed up with photographer Liora K and "traditionally attractive" Tucson model John Shay, and one morning we met at a photography studio where I took off my shirt (an Abercrombie one I had picked up, which, as a size "Large," weirdly fit) and got sexy with a guy that the world told me I couldn't.

After receiving the photos and superimposing in Times New Roman font the words "Attractive & Fat"—in a way strangely reminiscent of the A&F logo—onto the images, I wrote an open letter (that, thank god, was edited with the help of friends) to Jeffries and posted that shit to my blog and Facebook.

The letter read:

May 19, 2013

Mike Jeffries
c/o Abercrombie & Fitch
Abercrombie & Fitch Campus
6301 Fitch Path
New Albany, Ohio 43054

Hey Mike,
I know you've been flooded with mail regarding your
comments on sizeism, but I wanted to take a second to write
you about a project I've been working on.

As a preface: Your opinion isn't shocking; millions share the
same sentiment. You've used your wealth and public platform
to echo what many already say. However, it's important you
know that regardless of the numbers on your tax forms, your

comments don't stop anyone from being who they are; the
world is progressing in inclusive ways whether you deem it cool
or not. The only thing you've done through your comments
(about thin being beautiful and only offering XL and XXL in
your stores for men) is reinforce the unoriginal concept that
fat women are social failures, valueless, and undesirable. Your
apology doesn't change this.

   Well, actually, that's not all you have done. You have also
created an incredible opportunity for social change.
Never in our culture do we see sexy photo shoots that pair
short, fat, unconventional models with not short, not fat,
professional models. To put it in your words: "unpopular kids"
with "cool kids." It's socially acceptable for same to be paired
with same, but never are contrasting bodies positively mixed in
the world of advertisement. The juxtaposition of uncommonly
paired bodies is visually jarring, and, even though I wish it
didn't, it causes viewers to feel uncomfortable. This is largely
attributed to companies like yours that perpetuate the thought
that fat women are not beautiful. This is inaccurate, but if
someone were to look through your infamous catalog, they
wouldn't believe me.

   I've enclosed some images for your consideration. Please let
me know what you think.

   A note: I didn't take these pictures to show that the male
model found me attractive, or that the photographer found
me photogenic, or to prove that you're an ostentatious dick.
Rather, I was inspired by the opportunity to show that I am
secure in my skin and to flaunt this by using the controversial
platform that you created. I challenge the separation of
attractive and fat, and I assert that they are compatible
regardless of what you believe. Not only do I know that I'm
sexy, but I also have the confidence to pose nude in ways you
don't dare. You are more than welcome to prove me wrong by

posing shirtless with a hot fat chick; it would thrill me to see such a shoot.

I'm sure you didn't intend for this to be the outcome, but in many ways you're kind of brilliant. Not only are you a marketing genius (brand exclusivity really is a profitable move) but you also accidentally created an opportunity to challenge our current social construct. My hope is that the combination of these contrasting bodies will someday be as ubiquitous as the socially accepted ideal.

—Ever so sincerely,
Jes

P.S. If you would like to offer me a "substantial amount" to stop wearing your brand so my association won't "cause significant damage to your image," don't hesitate to email me. I respect you as a businessman, and my agent and I would be happy to contribute in furthering your established success. P.P.S. You should know your Large t-shirt comfortably fits a size 22. You might want to work on that.

Twelve hours later I was on a red-eye flight to New York City for an interview on *The Today Show*, and I then proceeded to spend the next twenty hours (no exaggeration there) in a hotel room doing interviews over the phone, Skype, and email for nearly every major news platform in the world. The world was outraged by the company's blatant exclusion, and people wanted to talk about it.

I loosely followed what happened to Abercrombie & Fitch afterwards. My campaign, along with a few others, was covered widely for a month, but didn't completely drop off as expected afterward—there were multiple follow-up articles written about A&F and how they were faring.

Here's the amazing part: A year later, they weren't faring well at all. Its downward-trending brand and closing stores, which had already started in 2013, only picked up speed as the negative press continued. Shareholders became hostile, and the masses? They were *angry* because of the exclusion. It was refreshing.

And now? Abercrombie & Fitch's stock is lower than it's been in *years*. I'm absolutely certain that many factors contributed to this, but it's possible that a large one was the everlasting outrage that remained in the headlines. For so long, in fact, that the company eventually made a paltry attempt to pacify and started carrying extra-large shirts for women. But by then shoppers were unconvinced: "They'll insult us and then *take our money*?"

Yeah, it didn't work.

This example of a dwindling corporation taken out by the public's general indignation is just too good to not share. It wasn't because of any one person; it was the power of the people that was the ultimate punch to the gut. Just as Shaer indicated in his article, we're becoming more inclusive and integrating diversity more than ever before. We have light-years to go, but I'm encouraged after seeing the failure of a company that beats its chest over its own harmful marketing tactics. Good job, consumers. You're making me proud.

Another interesting development within the fashion industry happened just as this book was going to print. Lane Bryant (the plus-size retailer) launched a "body positive" campaign called #ImNoAngel with six plus models who were "redefining sexy." The only issue? They were all that ubiquitous hourglass shape we discussed before. I decided that, once again, a counter campaign would be the ideal way to show both the company and consumer what an alternative ad *could* look like. I re-created the images with varying sizes of plus women who didn't necessarily fit the common model shape or "look." These photos were accompanied by a letter in which this was included:

> *I'm going to ask you to consider including some of the*
> *following next time: Cellulite; 90% of women have it. Bellies;*
> *many plus women don't have flat torsos. All abilities; we're*

all inherently sexy. Transgender women; they're "all woman"
too. Small boobs and wide waists; we're not all "proportional."
Stretch marks and wrinkles; they're trophies of a life lived. And
this is just the beginning! I've taken the liberty of creating some
inclusionary images with Jade Beall, reminiscent of yours.
These photos highlight all of these things mentioned above
... and y'know what? I find them sexy as hell. I believe that
constructive criticism is an important part of making progress,
but I also believe that when you attach a solution you've got a
game changer! Hopefully these can be a game changer for you.
Now, I realize that you are a company with financial motives
(and that change is often met with resistance), but if you're
truly interested in empowering all women and joining the body
positive conversation, I strongly suggest you consider widening
your definition of "sexy."

I have a feeling that because the letter was written to engage a company that had the ability to and voiced interest in changing the conversation (instead of shutting the dialogue down), a response landed in my inbox the next day. Lane Bryant's CEO Linda Heasley shared that she read the post many times and was appreciative of the opportunity to think, which for her, then instigates action. She also expressed gratitude for being pushed in a much-needed direction and agreed that Lane Bryant can do more towards building body confidence and encouraging inclusivity.

This made me fucking smile. Not because my images were perfect or included every marginalized body type (they weren't, and they didn't), or because now everything is all better (it's not), but because ... perhaps what I hoped for could still be possible: that we don't have to alienate those companies that have the ability to reach individuals whom activists can't, but we can still approach these companies with honesty and ask for change. If we're real with ourselves about how change is best achieved in this fucked-up world, we'll acknowledge that utopian ideals will *always* be the goal, but the steps toward this will be slow and far from perfect. This is common for all large contested movements, and there is *still* an overwhelming amount of societal pushback when it comes to visible body acceptance. Sometimes the most effective way of creating change is by breaking down old walls and dismantling social issues from the inside out, and I fully plan on doing this whenever the opportunity arises. Lane Bryant reaches many women who are still unfamiliar with the concept of body love, and I'm hoping that their small (or large?) changes will bring this idea to light for those who may find me too radical or abrasive. Will we see this change? Maybe. Maybe not. Retail has had a long-standing relationship with Exclusivity and I honestly just don't know. But even just having a conversation between consumers (the Internet and I) and a CEO (Linda) is progress.

So I'm hopeful.

And, guys, we NEED that hope, because even though we've made progress, we've still got a long way to go.

Case in point: I am notorious for complaining every summer as I search for sexy swimsuits for bigger gals, and I almost always end up banging my head against the wall at the inequality. There simply aren't as many options as there are for straight sizes, and much of the clothing that *is* available (especially in brick and mortar stores) is limited in style. And the swimsuits usually come with skirts. So what the fuck am I supposed to do if I don't like skirts?

Of course, this always prompts an even larger question for me: Why don't we see *more* plus clothes? We see some, but not enough. Why isn't the market for larger ladies who want to look amazing being recognized the same way the straight-sized market is? The answer is complex, but one large contributor is stigma, and the direct consequence is that there simply are not enough vendors to make and sell plus clothing. This is something I learned at a clothing company's launch event and something I've heard from other designers as well.

But here's the interesting thing: **Plus-size women have A LOT of buying power**. In fact, there are more size-16 women in the U.S.

than there are size 0 and size 2 combined, and lots of those women have dollars they wanna spend real bad.[5] Manufacturers are starting to realize this, so we are seeing a little bit of an increase in fashionable clothing, though not enough (and certainly not enough in the swimwear department—TARGET, I'M LOOKING AT YOU). But I'm pretty sure we can change this. I am convinced that a contributing factor (however small or large) to the lack of options is the fact that we're still not comfortable in our bodies. The demand for slimming-tucking-trimming-hiding-camouflaging clothing still outweighs the wear-whatever-we-want clothing, and this won't change until we use our buying power to show otherwise.

We need to show that WE LOVE OUR BODIES AND WE WANT ALL THE OPTIONS. We can do this by supporting companies that stylishly dress larger women (large brands, sure, but remember those kick-ass indie companies too!) by purchasing exactly what we want (the way we want), and by being vocal about what we'd like to see. Never underestimate the power of consumer demands; we have the ability to shift the fashion industry in a big way, as evidenced by both the Target boycott and the Abercrombie shitshow.

Oh god, fatshion is SO political.

But besides the larger picture of examining the policies of companies and corporations and big-box stores and giant malls . . . there is another way to use fatshion that I think is just as important: your daily outfit choices.

I love to share with people that a wonderful way to start the body love journey is to **wear what scares you.**

This has been one of the most transformative steps to feeling comfortable inside my body and with how it looks. A couple of years ago (along with the "25 things"), as a personal dare to myself, I decided to start wearing the things I'd always wanted to, but never had the *cojones* to. One summer I was especially inspired by a quote from a columnist from the *Boston Globe* who, discussing summer trends, writes:

> *I'm a firm believer that everyone should wear what makes*
> *them comfortable (in my case that happens to be a Slanket*
> *and tennis shoes), but I'm not a fan of any article of clothing*
> *that has the potential to show off muffin tops. There will be a*
> *contingent of women wearing them who shouldn't, and then*
> *a contingent of women who will wish they could wear them.*
> *And my deepest respect for the women who can wear these and*
> *actually pull them off.*[6]

Jezebel responded with, "May God save those fat women who dare to don crop tops without prior approval from the *Boston Globe*'s Christopher Muther."[7]

To which *I* said: Well, may god please save my sexy fat ass.

I LOVE a good challenge, and that summer it was ON: I donned my first-ever crop top, which highlighted the area of my body I've always hidden the most. I wore it out to get drinks with a friend, and it was the first time I stepped into the bustling community wearing less around my midriff. The breeze across my belly was initially shocking and uncomfortable. I couldn't get over the insatiable need to apologetically smile at everyone I walked past. "I'm sorry you can see my stomach!" and "I won't blame you for averting your eyes" were the things I had to stop my eyes from saying. But after time went on, my shame quickly transitioned into shameless empowerment, and that striped crop top became just the first little shirt of many that summer!

If you were to fast-forward and find me a year later, you'd be able to find me easily. I was the one on the fire escape on the third story of a NYC building in my underwear, posing while an audience below cheered me on. I then got fully naked and posed in the same window, all of this for the creator of the Adipositivity Project, Substantia Jones.

I know for a fact that that one brazen crop top led me (albeit in a series of small steps) to posing nude for all the world to see (I'm in calendars across the country!), and while this kind of bravery doesn't come overnight, it does come. Especially if you start to wear what scares you.

Fashion doesn't have to be fluff. When I shrugged off the fabricated *do*'s and *do not*'s, clothing started to embolden me. It started to empower me. And clothing is now my statement. It's a way that I say what I want, when I want, for no one save me. And THIS, my friends, is most certainly revolutionary.

One of my favorite quotes of all time is from Kirsty Fife, who says, "I now wear my clothes as a form of political resistance."[8]

When you are told that you are insignificant, inferior, not "cool" enough, unimportant, undeserving of representation; that you should hide, shrink, cover up, walk with your head down, and not take up space . . . to do the opposite of that is a radical and paradigm-changing action. Just do *you*. Stand out by wearing whatever the fuck you want. Wear the tutu. Wear the horizontal stripes. Wear the turquoise skinny jeans. Wear the see-through blouse. Wear the bikini. Wear the tie and vest. Wear the sweatpants. Wear the shirt that says, "Does this shirt make me look fat?" Wear whatever it is that makes you happy, because this is your life.

Wear what you love. Wear what speaks to you. Wear what scares you shitless. And see what it feels like to start your own revolution.

THE CASE FOR MALE FATSHION
BRUCE STURGELL OF CHUBSTR.COM

I started blogging out of frustration. As a "man of size," trying to find clothes that fit in the mainstream shops in my little Midwestern town was an exercise in futility. After a particularly unsuccessful (and mildly embarrassing) trip to the local mall, I ended up back at home, empty-handed and angry. I had money, I knew what I was looking for, but none of the clothes I wanted to wear were available in my size. I felt powerless. What could I do? I did the only thing I could think of—the thing most of us do these days: I headed to the Internet to bitch about it.

I went to Tumblr and created a blog with a basic, forgettable name. My entire plan at that point was to call out the brands that had forsaken me, and boy, were there a lot of them. I complained about the lack of options for guys my size, my horrible experiences with store employees who wanted nothing to do with me, and the fact that none of the brands I liked cared about catering to a plus-size male audience.

After a while, I realized I could complain AND do what some of the female body image sites were doing: put up "outfit-of-the-day" posts. I tried sharing a few photos, along with information on what I was wearing and where I bought it. I did it more for posterity, thinking it'd be nice to document the things I liked, and the things I didn't. It turns out that I was starting to create a resource others could use.

People started ACTUALLY READING what I was writing. Even more mind-blowing, people were asking for my advice on style, what to wear on a date, to an interview, even how to dress for a wedding. When these readers started sending me pictures, I realized there was an opportunity to create a real resource for men of size, and Chubstr was born.

Many men are taught that having feelings about their body image isn't . . . manly. It's not something to discuss, and it's not something to celebrate. We're supposed to focus on more masculine pursuits, and fashion isn't one of them. Being chronically pudgy adds another confusing dimension to these unspoken rules. Not only are you not supposed to care about style, but you have to be okay with being ridiculed for your size. If you want anything more than what society is willing to give you, you're reaching too far.

I was lucky to be raised in a family that valued creativity and individuality, that told me I was as good as anyone else, and encouraged me to strive for whatever it was I wanted. That helped keep me balanced from a very young age, and I believe it also led me to start Chubstr.

Chubstr has a mission statement: to help men of size find, create, and share their style with the world. When I started doing this, there just weren't any communities out there for guys like me. My goal was to create a website that presented big men in a positive light, with a level of professionalism on par with the *Esquire*s and *GQ*s of the world. While the professionalism isn't quite there, my hope is that we've created something that gents from all walks of life, ethnicities, and sizes can identify with.

I can see the positive change. Mainstream media is taking notice, and Chubstr is being featured by some of the most popular websites and newspapers in the world. We're getting opportunities to interview celebrities, and brands are coming to the site to get advice on the burgeoning men's plus-size industry. *Men's plus-size industry.* Is there such a thing? I guess so. In a few years, I think it'll be much more than Hawaiian shirts and *The Sopranos* tracksuits. There will be real, stylish options for men of a variety of sizes.

The best part of all of this? For me, it's the vibrant community that I've watched sprout up around Chubstr. People who, like me, had nowhere else to go—now they have an option. They have a resource and a safe place to go to ask questions, get advice, and be inspired by amazing photos of people who look like them, celebrating their personal style, whether they're size L or 8X.

Recognize that body image and style is an issue for big gents and want to help change things? Try these:

- **Lobby brands that don't currently offer clothing in extended sizes to consider doing so.** There's a demographic that is willing and eager to buy what they have to offer, if it's available in their size. Social media allows everyone's voices to be heard—use it to reach out to these companies.

- **Spread the word about positive online resources for men's plus-size style and body image.** You might even find that some of the women's plus-size bloggers you follow feature gents from time to time. Tell them you'd like to see more. If all else fails, I can think of one style site for the big-and-tall man that you can send people to. **Talk to the guys in your life about body image and style.** You might be surprised to find out that the guy you thought never cared about fashion doesn't care about it because he doesn't think there are any options out there for him. If the big guys you know are anything like I used to be, they don't know about or concern themselves with personal style because they're not seeing stylish guys that look anything like them in popular culture. At all. Talk to them, explain the resources available, and most of all, be open and helpful. People who haven't considered fashion before might not know where to start. You can help them by finding out what they like, what they hate, and who their style role models are. Then go out and help them recreate some of the looks that they like.

✳

affirmations aren't just for people who love sedona: you can rewire your brain

[CHAPTER ELEVEN]

A lot of times we assume that things like affirmations are *only* for people who love crystals, outdoor yoga, psychic wisdom, energy vortexes, and astrology. Y'know . . . like the people who love my fellow Arizonan city and wonderful epicenter of all things some people call "woo-woo," Sedona.

Me? I may not be interested in "vibrational matches," but I DO think that affirmations are the greatest fucking thing ever and that EVERYONE should give them a try. I'm talking everyone—including you—not just the New Age tourists. Though I understand if you're skeptical. I was too.

I Googled "why positive affirmations are important," hoping to find some concise inspiration on the subject that would help me explain it to you . . . but all the shit I found was the kind of stuff that makes my eyes start to glaze over so I squint at the words hoping they'll become helpful but then everything just gets blurry and all of a sudden I find myself reading "How to Organize Your Bathroom Vanity Like a Pro" on a lifestyle blog knowing goddamn well I'll never organize shit in my bathroom.

This is exactly the experience I'm trying to save you from. In a word, here's why positive affirmations are important: **neuroplasticity**.

And neuroplasticity is our friend.

Also called brain plasticity, neuroplasticity refers to our brains' ability to forge new neural connections and learn to think in new ways in response to changes in our behavior, emotions, environment, even our own new thoughts.[1]

The prevailing belief used to be that brains were static and didn't adjust as easily as we now know they do. We've since learned that our brains learn and form neural connections based on our experiences, and that, even when damage is done as a result of these experiences— when those connections are broken—the neurons in our brains can find ways to reconnect. Even though the brain is hardwired to remember negative interactions more than the positive ones (to help us survive the dangers of the world), we now understand that the higher regions of the brain can change how the lower regions function.[2] That, in the words of Daniel Pierce (yes, Daniel Pierce from the TV show *Perception*), "we can use our intention and our attention in sustained focused ways to overcome the brain's negative bias." And he's right. Rick Hanson, PhD, author of *Hardwiring Happiness: The New Brain Science of Contentment, Calm, and Confidence*, is all about helping brains retrain themselves and work toward hardwiring positivity when we get so stuck on negativity. Hanson backs me up that this isn't New-Agey gibberish in an online *Fast Company* article, which quotes him as saying, "This is not just 'smell the roses' . . . I am talking about positive neuroplasticity. I am talking about learning. . . . The brain is changing based on what flows through it."[3]

In short?

Our brains are fucking amazing, regenerating, retrainable, malleable machines.

We have learned to feel bad about ourselves through a lifetime of negative experiences. Think about it: As little kids, we thought our bodies were fucking fabulous (if you can't remember this for yourself, think of a child you know right now). We were in awe of the things our bodies could do. There was a discovery period in which there was nothing more amazing than this body we inhabited, and we were unashamed. We poked our skin, sucked on our toes, and showed our bellies unabashedly; we thought our bodies were hot shit.

> **Our brains are fucking amazing, regenerating, retrainable, malleable machines.**

And then something changed.

Somehow we transitioned into loathing our bodies. The wonder left and the hatred came to stay. We started to experience moments in when we experienced a negative reaction about our bodies from someone else. We started to learn that our bodies were bad, embarrassing, shameful, inferior . . . whatever the negative story was that the world taught us. And because our brains are so trainable, we believed those things. But it wasn't always this way.

Body hate isn't something we're born with. It's totally and completely learned.

The good news? Thanks to neuroplasticity, we can unlearn the hate and retrain our brains to see ourselves with love.

There's a really great and simple example of how this can be done.

It's called a Yay! Scale, and it was created by the Flabulous (her own words) Marilyn Wann. It's, yes, a bathroom scale, but it's not your typical scale. It's covered in iridescent silver contact paper (or maybe hot pink faux fur, if you get lucky when you order it at VoluptuArt.com) but it also has something else . . .

All the numbers have been replaced with adjectives that tell you how bangin' you actually are. Instead of seeing your weight in pounds you see words like "sexy," "lovely," "hot," "perfect," "adorable" . . . on

THE FAT PEOPLE: *do all the things!* CHALLENGE ✳

#10: ROLL DOWN A HILL.

I seriously don't understand why fat people shouldn't do this, unless you're allergic to grass. People can be so weird.

Your challenge: If you're not allergic, DO IT. Go to the park. Bring bubbles and balloons. Swing on those swings. Have a picnic and roll down the motherfucking hill like you just don't care. Be five years old again and have *fun!*

and on. And while this is quite kitschy and makes a perfect novelty gift, it's so much more.

In our world, we have developed a bad case of what Golda Poretsky calls "scale-dependent self-esteem" (watch her TEDx video, "Why It's Okay to Be Fat"—WATCH IT).[4] The whole point of getting on the scale is usually when you're on a "diet" and/or to see how you're doing weight-wise. Are you doing well? Or poorly? We step on the scale and our mood shifts one way or the other depending on what the numbers say. If we step on the scale and we've lost a pound? The world is ours. If we step on the scale and the number goes up? We crumble. We feel sad, maybe we feel like a failure; it suddenly feels like a hard day; our goal of becoming a "better version" of ourselves is shot. The positive is short-lived, and the negative sets in . . . every time this happens, we feel it. Hard. And because our brains are wired to hold on to the negativity, the feelings we remember more often are feelings of sadness and failure.

Step on a scale every day for a year (or thirty), be publicly weighed at school, join a weight loss-based group, and your association with that tool will likely be negative and crushing to your self-esteem. You're gonna hate the scale.

What Marilyn has so brilliantly created with her Yay! Scale is a way to re-wire that thinking. On this scale, you step on it (I was terrified the first time I tried!) and you look down . . . and it tells you that you're RAVISHING.

You.

Ravishing.

At this weight.

Quit looking around, yes, you.

It's a totally foreign experience and one that doesn't match up with your past experiences with a scale. It tells you that you're ravishing and shows you that ravishing-ness doesn't need to align with a number to be so. You're ravishing no matter what the number is.

You just had a positive experience with a negative association.

And if you were to step onto this scale and see these positive terms as many times as you've stepped onto a regular scale? Well, I bet you'll have a different relationship with your Yay! Scale than you have with the one currently in your bathroom. Oh, by the way: Throw out that fucking scale and replace it with Marilyn's already.

It's almost TOO simple, but trust me, it works.

ALSO, while I think Yay! Scales are awesome and every house would be *way* cooler with one of these in them, you actually don't need anything other than a piece of paper and a pen to try rewiring your brain in your own life. I'm about to give you what I call "The Post-it Challenge."

You can use a Post-it and a marker, or any piece of paper and a pen. Lipstick and a mirror. Sharpie and a wall (don't tell your landlords I okayed that). Whatever you have, you can use it for this challenge.

Here's what I want you to do.

The Post-it Challenge

STEP 1: THINK OF SOMETHING YOU LOVE ABOUT YOUR BODY.

One thing you love about your body—could be *anything*. I love my hair. My legs are strong. The freckle on my back is cute. My body gave birth to my child. My skin regenerates. I love my rockin' tits. My toes are adorable. My ass is so spankable. I love the way there's that curve on my side. My legs let me dance. My arms can lift heavy things. My body heals itself. Whatever your version is, find one thing. If you can't find even one thing that you love about your body, that's okay. Head to the next step anyway.

STEP 2: NEXT, THINK OF AN AFFIRMATION.

An affirmation is *a declaration of something that is true and used to practice positive thinking.* This is the part where affirmations aren't weird and not just for people who love chanting; in fact they're pretty damn fun and for absolutely everyone.

Some examples of affirmations could be: My body is beautiful; my mind is brilliant. I LOVE me. I acknowledge my own self-worth. I am perfect and complete just the way I am. My body deserves love. Girl, you are KILLIN' it today! I release myself from outside expectations.

Others that I have heard and loved: My hair is gray and that's more than okay. I am worthy of love. It is okay to love myself just as I am. My body is a vessel of awesomeness. Goddamn, I'm hot shit. This is my life and I have decided that my body is good.

My personal choice? *I am okay.*

For me, a simple "You are okay, Jes" is all I need. I challenge you to find one that speaks to you, whatever that may be.

STEP 3: WRITE DOWN YOUR AFFIRMATION AND THAT THING YOU LOVE ABOUT YOUR BODY.

It's great that you've found your affirmation (and if someone is around, tell them what you've decided!), but make sure you write it on that Post-it Note (or piece of paper, or mirror). Place your affirmation wherever you tend to be when you have the most negative thoughts. It could be your bathroom mirror, your bedroom or the room where you get dressed every day, next to or under your pillow so it's there when you go to sleep and when you wake up. You know where those spiraling thoughts most often come; put your Post-it (or whatever) there.

STEP 4: EVERY TIME YOU HAVE A NEGATIVE THOUGHT, I WANT YOU TO READ YOUR POST-IT OUT LOUD.

Don't skim it. Don't read it in your head. Read it *and* say it out loud. Here's why it's important that you do so: When you're having a negative thought and you say a positive thought out loud, it is impossible for the negative thought to remain. They simply can't coexist in the same place at the same time. So you're ridding your brain of the old way of thinking; you're ejecting the toxic shit and forcefully jump-starting it into a positive direction. And your brain never had a chance to say no.

You get to be totally in control, and you get to say the truth even when the lies seem so loud.

Try doing this for weeks, or maybe even months.

See what happens.

Affirmations are for everyone, because positive thinking is for everyone. Body love is for everyone. Self-esteem is for everyone.

And that includes you.

*

fat girls find love, too: yes, that includes you

[CHAPTER TWELVE]

Here is the BIGGEST MYTH in all of Fat Girl mythdom: Fat girls never find love.

On this, I call *bullshit*, my dear friends. The bulliest shit there is.

Fat girls find ALL KINDS of love! They find community love. Instant love. Friend love. Kitten love. Family love. Work love. Puppy love. Partner love. Lover love. Coffee date love. Lifetime-forever love. And yes, most importantly, they find self-love.

Pfft.

Never find love, my ass.

Community and Friend Love

I'm learning so much about the power that having a circle of friends can hold in my life. Not just one friend, or a bunch of acquaintance friends, but rather a tight-knit circle of people who know you, love you, and support you. It's a fucking wonderful thing.

It's also a fucking *important* thing.

Obviously, who you surround yourself with matters, and when you're learning to love yourself (and your body), it's critical to be around those who are aligned with your values and supportive of your ultimate goals. Take inventory of those around you. Make sure they respect themselves *and* you. Make sure they are the kinds of people who are working toward happiness. Make sure the good they bring is good, and the bad they bring is far less than the good.

A favorite tweet of mine?

> @VirgieTovar: *Envision the life you want. Find the people who will help you create that life. Love them unconditionally. Repeat.*

That's from my gal Virgie Tovar, of course.

We are taught to be nice and polite humans, and that those who in any way disregard others *must* lack some sort of moral upbringing. We are also conditioned to believe that the more people like us, the better. As in, the closer your individual "feedback" rating is to 100 percent, the better a person you are. This is sometimes called the "Need-to-Please Disease," and there are a number of causes. It's especially common with those of us who have super low self-esteem. When we don't believe in ourselves, we think we need a large number of other people to validate us. Unfortunately, while support systems are definitely necessary, accumulating copious amounts of devotees ain't the answer. We don't need a million friends; we need a few great ones. If you find yourself struggling with the Need-to-Please Disease, try spending less time trying to seduce lots of people to "like" you and instead focus on cultivating relationships with those who are also working toward a life full of love, happiness, and (most importantly) progress.

Now, I'm not saying you should ditch any of your friends who aren't wildly successful and spout affirmations every ten seconds with a shit-eating grin on their faces 24/7.

In fact, if you had friends like that, I would be completely weirded out and wonder what they're hiding, because Jesus, whatever it is, it must be BIG.

What I AM trying to say is probably better said by Jade Beall:

Find a community that can see YOU! Don't hang out with people who are obsessing about how they need to be different to be happy. Find people who are happy, or are at least practicing happiness as they are now so that they can infect you with their happiness and you can infect them with yours. I stopped hanging out with people who complain about themselves all the time, and it's a work in progress; a practice. But I want to be around those who work toward self-love instead of self-hatred. I have enough of that on my own.

Yes. That.

There are, of course, ways to find a middle ground if you're not sure what's best for you OR if you're not wanting to go out and find a whole slew of new relationships right now. If your friend says something degrading about you, try responding, "Jesus, that really hurt my feelings, and I would prefer that you stop commenting negatively about me, kthx." Or, if your friends are endlessly "diet talking" about how they could *never* eat that or how they feel so *fat OMG*, try redirecting the conversation to another topic, or say something like, "I'd really prefer we talk about something else. So how about that last episode of 'How to Get Away with Murder'?" or whatever neutral topic you like.

What if you don't have any body positive friends, and when you say, "Please don't make fun of my body," they say, "Fuck you, loser!"? Well (obvs), ditch 'em, and find positive support elsewhere.

A word (or four hundred) on losing friends: Whether they leave you or you leave them, it can be an emotional and difficult experience. But let me remind you of something: Every friend and loved one in our lives holds a different role, and they each stay for a certain period of time. Tyler Perry's character Madea (of ALL people) gave some incredible advice about this in the film *Madea Goes to Jail*. She talks about how some people come into our lives for a long time, maybe even our whole lives, and some people are "seasonal"—they only stay for a period of time, and it's imperative that we don't confuse these types of people and their roles. Along the same lines, she says some people are like leaves; they are easily blown around—they don't offer much, and are unreliable. I'm gonna be real with you right now: Most people are leaves. And just like Madea says, that's okay. Just acknowledge that they're a leaf and move on.

Then the Madea character goes on to say that some people are like branches, and branches are to be cautiously approached. They may look strong, but as soon as you try to lean on them for support, "they'll break and they'll leave you high and dry." All you need, she says, is a few people to be your roots.[1] THOSE people are the ones who will nourish you and be there for the long haul, and once you find 'em? Keep 'em.

The rest of them? Let 'em go.

Here's the beautiful thing: When you let these people go, whether you realize at the time that they're toxic or you don't see how they brought negativity until they're gone . . . you're making space for new things. **It's so important to make space for new things.**

I know this may sound strange, but if you've made some space and need some emotional or body encouragement *now* . . . you can find it in books. Believe me when I tell you that books can be your best friend. Remember in Chapter 8 where I talked about the five-legged stool? For me, one of those legs has always been uplifting literature and nonfiction. If you're looking for suggestions, there are many in the back of this book. There were three books that became my besties through thick and thin: *Hot and Heavy: Fierce Fat Girls on Life, Love & Fashion*, edited by Virgie Tovar (Seal Press, 2012), *Lessons From the Fat-o-sphere: Quit Dieting and Declare a Truce with Your Body*, by Kate Harding and Marianne Kirby (Perigee Books, 2009), and *Fat! So?:*

Because You Don't Have to Apologize for Your Size, by Marilyn Wann (Ten Speed Press, 1998). These books inspired the shit out of me when I first read them, and continue to do so every time I pick them up. If you're all out of resources or people to turn to for support, try this. See if it doesn't help.

We only have so much space in our lives, in our homes, our hearts and our brain. If we fill that space with meaningless knick-knacks, subpar friends, and negative thoughts . . . we don't have room for anything else.

So clear that unproductive clutter out. And open yourself up to bigger and better things. It won't happen until you make room, so get on it. And let in only the people and things that propel you toward a happier and more inspirational life, because that's what you deserve.

Let everything else go.

Partner Love

Over the last few years, I've received countless letters, read hundreds of comments, and listened to many, many, many women (and men) speak about their fear that they might never find love . . . all because of their bodies.

It's heartbreaking to hear, but god, how I get it. I've totally been there too.

I know that hopelessness. The resignation to a life without. I know the things you tell yourself to make it seem not so bad. The blind eye you turn to the happiness around you because it's too painful to watch. I know the promises you make to yourself—promises that you'll change your body so you can *become* lovable. I know the anger that then rises up because, WAIT A MINUTE! *I shouldn't have to change my body to be loved!* But that realization is quickly overshadowed by a lifetime of shame that comes sweeping back, and you once again buy the lie that you must change "for the better." You believe, deep down, that to be desirable you must fix yourself. I know this exhausting tug-of-war between wanting to be loved as you are but also just wanting to be loved by anyone at all. It fucking sucks.

But, while on this body acceptance journey, I've learned many many *many* wonderful truths, and there is one in particular that has changed every facet of my life. It goes against everything we've been told (and I kind of already gave it away), but it's still as true as ever. **Fat girls find love too.**

They find the whole-mother-fucking-package kind of love. The no-holds-barred, every-inch-of-you-is-perfect, kisses-on-what-you-thought-was-un-kissable, lifetime-of-yesses, lusting, loving, dedicated-for-life kind of love. It happens. Often, and everywhere.

You might wonder why this section of the "love chapter" is a million miles long. "HEY JES aren't community and self-love important too?" Well, hell yeah! Just as much, if not more so! But if there is one thing that I have really struggled with feeling unworthy of, been told I'll never find . . . it's partner love.

When all we want as humans is to feel loved, be seen, and have a partner (or five or ten) to spend our time with . . . and then we're told we'll never have it simply because of our bodies? Well, to set that bullshit straight is gonna take me more than a few pages to refute.

Now, I've been in terrible, horrible, no good, very bad relationships . . . just like everyone else. You know the kind. The relationships that end with you on the couch dangerously bargaining with yourself, trying to convince god-knows-who that you'll make it right. *It will be fine if I lose weight. If I make changes he/she/they will stay. Those changes are worth a relationship, right? I'll just get skinnier . . . they'll stay and everything will be better.* You sit on that couch thinking you can strike a deal with the Weight Loss Devil and that it will somehow save your relationship, even though there were countless other red flags along the way. These red flags ran much deeper than your looks (and you most likely knew a long time ago that it wouldn't work out with this person), but in this moment you have decided that the inevitable failure has everything to do with your body. Because, yes, a lot of us find ourselves

THE FAT PEOPLE: *do all the things!* CHALLENGE *

#11: RUN.

This is a pretty loaded "shouldn't."

I love to bash fatty myths, so let's lay this one out to dry: The idea that all large people are sedentary and live a life void of exercise is a load of baloney. Throughout my online travels, I've gotten to know many advocates who live a physically rigorous lifestyle, and many of them teach movement as well. Louise Green is a perfect example, and one of my favorite humans. She is a proud plus athlete who runs a training program called Body Exchange and is constantly participating in half marathons as well as hiking the North Shore mountains in Canada. She is fit and fat, which is more common than you might believe.

The interesting part about this "shouldn't" is that public consensus says fat people should just exercise more to become skinnier, yet we're apparently not allowed to run, jump, bicycle, dance, or work out. Hmmm. To be clear: No one is obligated to exercise (like, ever), but we are also allowed to move our bodies any way we damn well please. Endorphins are not just for the "worthy" group.

Your challenge: Go for a jog. Be sure to tell your family that you love them first though . . . just in case you internally combust while running. Because, y'know . . . fat people doing any form of exercise "just ain't *natural*." (Eye roll.) Now go kick some ass! Run off into the sunset with a final yell of "LATER, HATERS!"

with toxic individuals (OMG, especially me—the *doozies* I've stayed with FOR YEARS), believing that emotional abuse or detachment is just part of the package. That we are lucky to have someone at all. That this was as good as it could get. That we should be grateful for the companionship because who else could ever love our imperfect body? Have you been there? Fucking-A. Me too.

It was only at the end of the last painful breakup that I realized **this loveless relationship wasn't something I deserved.** I didn't deserve it, and its failure had nothing to do with my body. His inability to have a relationship was not a judgment on my figure. It wasn't a sign of my worth. And it wasn't something I needed to fix.

> I made an agreement with myself that I was worthy of total and complete love without changing anything for anyone.

In that moment I made an agreement with myself that *I was worthy of total and complete love without changing anything for anyone.* I wasn't going to change my morals, ethics, views on happiness . . . and most of all, I wasn't going to change my body.

After that decision, things shifted. I started dating. A lot. And this led to an even **bigger** revolutionary realization.

I am not limited by my body when it comes to whom I can date.

I wholeheartedly believed that it was impossible for a short and fat (or other socially shunned body type) woman like me to date a not-short, not-fat (or other socially worshipped body type) man that I was interested in.

This. Is. A. Total. Lie.

I quickly began to realize that my options are not limited because of my size. I had been under the assumption that I was not welcome to approach just *any* man; I had learned that I was to only engage with those who are as "socially unacceptable" as I thought I was. And yes, I find those bodies attractive as well, but the limiting, body-based exclusion seemed to be a glaring hurdle as I found myself newly single and presented with the dating world once again. Once I started to meet more men, however, I quickly learned: All those rules about sexual attraction that I internalized my entire life? Yeah, those were made up.

Totally and completely.

Maybe you already know this. Maybe this didn't slap you in the face like it did me, but it shocked, stunned, and thrilled me beyond belief. I COULD DATE ALL THE PEOPLE.

It turns out that no body is inferior (and consequently no body is superior), so *all bodies* have the opportunity to be paired with *all bodies*. This isn't an opinion. This is a fact. I see it in my life. I see it in other people's lives. I see it everywhere.

Everywhere except in what those advertising people produce.

Fuck those guys.

With this shining new epiphany I started to paint the town RED. I was not only armed with the knowledge that my dating options just expanded tenfold, but also armed with the confidence that my body wasn't "bad" and "undesirable" as I had thought for . . . y'know . . . my entire life.

I don't know if there are words for how powerful that epiphany really was.

Feeling emboldened and untouchable with my new secret discovery, I created a new purposefully unapologetic online dating handle. I made a profile under the name "SexyAndFat" and then proceeded to post full-body pictures. Lots of them. From all angles. I fell in love with dating online, and would casually check my inbox and filter through the hundreds of requests to select my dates for that week. After being in a horrific long-term relationship and also being chained to the *idea* that I wasn't deserving of attention and happiness (and sex!), I had decided that I was going to soak up all the attention, happiness, and sex I wanted.

I started to do what made ME feel like a babe on dates. I dressed up in miniskirts and fishnets when I wanted to and I dressed down in a t-shirt and jeans if I felt like it. I no longer felt that I needed to compensate for my size. WHAT A FUCKING CONCEPT.

I accepted attention, respect, and adoration. I had decided that I was okay, and therefore I was. I worked on my emotional well-being. I surrounded myself with incredible people. I dated a different person every day when it felt right. I also dated just one person, or no people, whenever *that* felt right. I had finally realized that I was not only worth people's time, I was also desirable, sexy, and totally and completely okay.

My body advocacy skyrocketed. I started traveling. Loving. Engaging. Giving. Receiving. Saying yes to the excellent and no to the less-than-average. I started to love myself unconditionally.

Sure, there were the usual ebbs and flows of dating, which for me usually looked like a couple of months of *OMG SO MANY DATES THIS IS SO FUN* followed by months of *Jesusgod THERE IS NO ONE in this town I wanna stick it out with*. But after a (long) while, a very sexy guy came into the picture (in all his fucking magical glory), and we clicked so hard it hurt. It was all there. We had chemistry. We knew how to respect others. We were both capable of epic communication. We gave only genuine compliments (which gave me soulgasms). We had fun nights followed by serious nights followed by ridiculously silly nights. We discussed progressive and hot topics and would also entertain ourselves for hours acting out what we thought my cats were thinking. There was patience, balance, human compassion, and really fucking hot sex. Our Venn diagrams overlapped PERFECTLY.

I have a guess as to why the timing was just so. Why this gem of a guy didn't come before the last boyfriend, and why he didn't show up when I first started dating after the breakup. It has something to do with this marvelous quote by Stephen Chbosky in his *The Perks of Being a Wallflower*: **"We accept the love we think we deserve."**[2] And boy, do we ever.

If I had met him before the last boyfriend, or just after the breakup, we might have hung out. Maybe. Maybe we'd have played pool and drunk wine and possibly have gotten frisky. But it wouldn't have worked, and it certainly wouldn't have lasted. Because back then I didn't believe I was worthy of something so genuinely wonderful. Back then I don't think I knew what genuinely wonderful even looked like.

The relationship I have now with that very sexy guy is still beautiful and solid. Of course, it isn't perfect (because no one's is, silly); I have my baggage and he has his, but our baggage mixes and matches perfectly . . . it looks really cute together. I'm happy about our cute, magic baggage every fucking day. And what if this relationship were to end? Well, then I'd find another wonderful connection that also has the respect, admiration, and joy I now know I deserve.

But while I've been cruisin' on this newfound love boat, much of the world has remained unaware of what I discovered in my epiphany. They still think that fat chicks are limited in who they date/marry/bang/love. I suppose I can see why; everywhere we go we are only shown couples that pair like bodies together. TV's *Mike and Molly*? A perfect example of a couple we don't find *too* surprising because they're both social pariahs, and therefore the attraction is socially acceptable. And we see the pairing of straight-sized bodies with straight-sized bodies . . . well, everywhere else. Movies. Television. Perfume ads. Everywhere. What this means is that when the world sees the *phenomenon* of a straight-sized person in love and lust with a fat person (as is the case with my boy and me), they are either blown away to the point of fascination (cue "mixed-weight relationship" TV shows) or they're freaked out and then quickly proceed to act like assholes.

The mixed-weight-relationship shows are frustrating, but *I really dislike* that asshole reaction, because it creates a larger issue beyond hating a fat body. **That issue being? The way these people proceed to shame the men who find themselves attracted to or dating women with atypical body types in our fat-phobic society**.

When the world looks at a "sexy" man with a fat woman, there are many assumptions: that he is settling. That he would prefer something else, but is forced to date a lesser lady. That he has a questionable fetish. That he is a perverse abomination. That when it comes to his sexual preference, there is something inherently wrong.

(I'm mentioning heterosexual men in this instance because we expect them to follow all social rules—dating included—without exception. Those with what the world considers "alternative preferences" have already broken "traditional protocol" and therefore receive significant ridicule in additional ways.)

Any body can be paired with any body. Fat with fat. Thin with thin. Fat with thin. Thin with fat. And everything in between.

This may seem obvious, but it's something that our culture struggles with on a fundamental level.

I had an experience a while back where I was out with my boy one night (looking hot as shit, I might add), and as we headed back to our bikes, someone (I'll call him Stupidly Drunk Dude) accosted My Him with the jeering question, "So, you're out hunting for cellulite tonight?"

Guys, I rarely get angry about this sort of criticism; I'm the proud recipient of copious amounts of hate mail, often with the subject line: "You're fat and ugly and an embarrassment to society." This ignorant opinion rolls off my back easily nowadays, but for some reason, this particular experience made me mad.

It could have been because I was already in the midst of a bad body day when it happened. Or maybe it's because after my boyfriend retorted, Stupidly Drunk Dude followed us down the avenue shouting a slew of horrid homophobic remarks at him. Or maybe my anger ignited because my boyfriend was rudely pulled into the ugly world of fat discrimination that I live in daily, but in which I protectively feel he doesn't belong. It could have been the fact that the comment came from a man and was said to my man, and this somehow made it hurt more. Or maybe it's just because it brought up a lot of shame in regard to a subject I feel passionately about: how unaccepting our world is of the pairing of traditionally attractive bodies with nontraditional ones.

Many (shall I say evolved?) people had previously adored our pairing (strangers gave us flowers and wine just because!), so even though it wasn't the first time we had experienced the opposite type of reaction, that night of street harassment was still really shitty. My gut reaction was overwhelming insta-shame—I found myself so self-conscious and irrationally afraid that my boy would all of a sudden realize that I was FAT, now that it was pointed out to him, and become ashamed of his choices. But real talk: He's already aware of this fact. Duh, right? He's seen it and he loves it. Not because I'm a novelty. Not because I'm a fetish. But because he simply finds me attractive as I am; it's that simple.

So make no mistake: I have a *fat body* that is often worshipped, but I am not necessarily worshipped for my *body fat*. For people to find my body attractive is not unusual, strange, or bothersome. And it is most certainly not a sign of mental instability. Finding me gorgeous doesn't automatically mean people have a fat fetish or an issue with their sexuality. It can mean that I'm simply sexy and people recognize that. I am so much more than an object for specific obsession.

So goddamnit, world, let the "odd" pairings be. Just because you may not prefer larger women doesn't mean there is something wrong with those who do, and the people who do like larger women deserve the opportunity to express this and act on it without the public shame they often receive. The reality is, a person's opinion and worth is not to be questioned or determined by the size of his partner's waist. So get the fuck over it.

Cleared that up? Good.

So, back to the really important real talk: All bodies can find partner love. And honestly, guys, they already do. While many people post comments that they're afraid they'll never find someone, twice as many comment about how sexy their husbands/wives/lovers think they are and how ecstatic they are to have unconditional love.

Now don't misunderstand. You *don't* have to have a partner to be happy. You don't have to have a lover to be lovable. You don't have to be paired up with someone else to be complete. Life is joyous and exciting and beautiful on our own as well. HOWEVER, if that is what you want . . . it can be yours regardless of your body type, and there is proof all around you if you look for it.

You CAN have it all.

Just the way you are right now. If you feel like there isn't hope, and you may never find the person you dream of . . . believe me (and believe the statistics) when I say that there is, and you can.

Self-Love

This is the shortest section about love, but not because it's unimportant. Oh, no. Just the opposite. It isn't ten pages long because at this point you don't need to read about self-love. You gotta get out there and practice some self-love.

No amount of education or research will do this for you. Sure, knowing critical things like how to stand up to companies, how to take care of our brains, how diversifying your media feed creates normalcy, how to take selfies so you can create your own narrative, and why we've learned to hate our bodies are all important. But once you know those things, you have to *go out there* and write a letter to that company, take care of your brain, follow those Tumblr sites, post your selfies, start loving your body, because history isn't reason enough not to, and you have to start all of that . . . now.

This whole BOOK is about self-love: loving your body and brain, and unapologetically loving your life. You just have to get out there and do it for yourself.

Easier said than done, huh? Yeah. I know.

Sometimes it's hard to find the internal push to rid ourselves of harmful thoughts, whatever they may be, so that we can continue with healthy actions. To help reverse negative patterns of behavior, there is a special kind of therapy called dialectical behavioral therapy (DBT). Created by Marsha M. Linehan, PhD, DBT is often taught in group settings, but it's also available in book form.

DBT suggests that you can work backward, using healthy actions to eliminate harmful thoughts. And because the brain and body are connected . . . it works. Kind of like a legitimate "fake it till you make it" concept, except way more useful.

One of the many tools Dr. Linehan created as part of DBT is called **opposite action**, which I have found to be useful in almost every facet of my life. The basic concept goes like this: If you are grappling with a negative emotion, one that you simply can't change no matter how hard you mentally arm-wrestle yourself . . . change your actions instead.[3]

Opposite action involves doing the opposite of your urges in the moment you are feeling that emotion. Linehan writes: "The idea behind this technique is that it can help to deal with distressing emotions by setting into motion an action that is helpful, not harmful."[4] This concept is critical for those who need a quick redirection of an emotion that is hurting them.

Opposite action doesn't work if you're trying to get rid of an emotion that is actually justified in the moment. Rather, it's a tool to bring you out of an *unwanted* emotion that is *unjustified* in the situation by replacing it with the emotion that is opposite—through action rather than trying to directly change what you're feeling. For example: If we are feeling shameful, our inclined action might be to stay indoors and sit with our shame alone (my therapist calls this "turtling"). If we know this isn't healthy for us, but we feel unable to change our feelings, then we can decide to change our actions. The opposite action being to leave our house (even for a moment) and perhaps interact with a friend. By doing so we won't escalate or heighten our feelings but rather help the feelings decrease by putting a countering action in their place.

Note, though: when we use opposite action our goal isn't to subdue our feelings, but instead to bring about a slow and steady change in those feelings by focusing on the actions themselves.

It seems simple and obvious, but you'd be surprised how often the opportunity arises for us to use opposite action, yet instead we stay stuck in the unwanted feeling. My point in going into all this is: If you're having a hard time with self-love and you just can't feel good no matter how hard you try . . . try changing the action you're naturally inclined to take. Outwardly love yourself so hard that you can't help but feel it on the inside. Treat your body well. Tell it that it's beautiful.

Wear what it loves to wear. Take it places it wants to go. Shower it with affection, smiles, kindness, and gratitude. Love yourself SO MUCH that you think, "Huh. I guess I must be lovable!"

That's how it starts. And then, with continued self-affection and rigorous positive self-talk . . . just watch. It will change everything.

You are worthy.

You are lovable.

You are perfect.

Your body is not a barrier to finding any kind of love, and you can *most definitely* have it all.

HOW TO HAVE HOT FAT SEX OR AS I LIKE TO CALL IT, "SEX"

CHRYSTAL BOUGON OF CURVY GIRL LINGERIE

I know. Everyone wants the secrets, right? How to have sex while fat. If you're not fat, you may wonder, "Is having fat sex different?" If you are fat, you may wonder, "Is having thin sex different?"

My guess is NO. There's not a lot of difference. Sure, maybe some positions may need some tweaking, but my guess is that it's all pretty much the same.

I mean, I can only speak for myself. I have had a "fat" body (according to the BMI and pretty much all of America's and insurance companies' standards) since I was eleven. I have been a fat person since I was in the third grade. I lost my virginity when I was nineteen. I have been a size 18 or larger since 1987. So, I can only speak for my own experiences.

We're all experiencing the same self-confidence issues. We're all nervous about being in crazy positions in the middle of the day with the lights on. I promise you, many women who are size 0 to size 8 have just as many insecurities as the rest of us. Fat men and women do not have a corner on the low self-esteem market. Lack of sexual confidence and being über-self-conscious **IS the human condition**. And you might also be surprised to know that men are self-conscious about their bodies, too. Men get overlooked so often when it comes to this topic of body image. Seriously. Many men are insecure about their bodies, their penis size, their love handles. It is a HUMAN thing to worry about your body and how it looks to someone else that you care about.

Okay, so what can we do as fat, thick, curvy women? How can we make sure we are getting the most out of our sex lives? How can we make it better? How can we turn it up? How can we leave our self-doubt about our rolls, stretch marks, and fat bodies at the door of our boudoir and really have some fun?

For one thing, just speaking logically and in the interest of keeping it very, very real, if your lover has gone out on a date or two or three with you and still wanted to go to bed with you—shouldn't that be enough validation that they are into you? Again, speaking for myself, I am a size 22 top and a size 22/24 pants. No matter how much I try to "dress for my shape" and wear styles that are flattering on my body (according to the people who make those rules), there is no camouflaging or covering up the fact that my body still takes up the space of a person who wears a size 22/24. As I like to say at my boutique, no matter how much black you wear, we can still tell how fat you are.

I also like to remind others, if someone keeps showing up naked in your bed with you over and over and over . . . that person is into you! That person is into your body exactly as it looks right this very second. They do not care that your arm fat is swinging back and forth or that you have stretch marks on your inner thighs. This person has chosen to be naked with you. What more do you need to know?

I have been educating and entertaining women and couples about sex toys and sex since 2003. I have talked to thousands of people about their sex lives, and they have shared so many intimate details with me. I can tell you it is a HUGE honor and privilege that so many people have confided in me. And do you know the one most common question I get from all the men I have talked to? "How can I get my wife/girlfriend to let go and have more fun?" I have met women who have asked me the same question about their wives or girlfriends. There are so many couples who want the other person to open up and let go more, to not be afraid to ask for what they want or to ask for something new and fresh. Yet so many people can't.

And this isn't exclusive to straight relationships. It happens to everyone. We get shy. We get in our own heads. We are so sure our lover is going to reject us for something that we consider to be an imperfection or defect. We are sure they are going to judge us and reject us because of our fat ass or our jiggly tummy . . . so we play it safe. But if you want to have HOT SEX, it takes communication and the ability to open up through communication. We fat girls have very thick skin because of all of the hatred we have received over the years about our bodies. So we can get very closed off—we work hard at protecting our hearts and our egos.

The truth is, the other person in your bed is just so happy that you want to have SEX with them that they aren't focused on your imperfections. They are INTO you, and into the fact that you are into them sexually. Live out loud and let go of your insecurities, and that is when your sex life can become smoking hot. It's when you are ready to be NAKED in the emotional way as well as the physical way that it gets really good.

You can try to hit all the right angles so your lover doesn't see your gut. And you can try to wear just the right lingerie or panties that cover your lower tummy or your stretch marks. (I hear it constantly at our plus-size lingerie boutique. "Do you have panties or lingerie I can wear WHILE we have sex so my stretch marks and tummy are covered?" And if it makes you feel better to wear something that covers up what you consider to be your flaws, then, yes—go for it. But I seriously doubt that is going to make your lover any hotter for you. They are going to be hot for you because you are hot for them. End of story. (All of that hiding and finding the right angles is so exhausting. I know. Been there. Done that.)

I think the best way to have hot sex is to check all that baggage at the door of your boudoir, or wherever you are getting busy, and remember that person CHOSE to be there with you. They are likely in their own head about their own shit that they are self-conscious about. GO WITH IT. Let go. The best sex is when you can turn off all of those old "tapes" in your head, the ones where you pick yourself apart. Those do not serve you in any way. Well, they **do not serve you in a healthy way**. Get rid of them. Erase them. Replace them with some good shit like "I LOVE MY FAT ASS" and "My body is hot." Because if *you* think your body is hot and ready for some red hot lovin', so will your partner.

Now go have some hot sex please . . . fat sex. Skinny sex. Thick sex. Queer sex. Straight sex. Plush sex. All other kinds of sex. It's all just SEX: two (or more!) humans enjoying each other's beautiful bodies and giving each other as much pleasure as possible.

*

loving your body will change the world

[CHAPTER THIRTEEN]

Here's a little pro tip:
It's really important to remember that it's okay to have days when you don't love yourself.

In fact, while I was writing this book I had many (*many*) horrible body days, one of which was so devastating that I felt unable to function and most certainly unable to look in the mirror. The ironic part? That particular day fell on a trip where I was headed to lecture a group of students on why loving your body is important and ten ways to do it. Those ten things? I do them religiously. And I STILL have horrible body days.

There's a quote I make everyone I know read that comes from coach and writer Mara Glatzel:

It's hard to be a fat girl. No matter how much you tell yourself how sexy, talented, amazing, worthy, fabulous, and genius

*you are, there is some pretty serious backlash you are facing
on a minute to minute basis. And, I'll tell you, I consider
myself pretty tough and persistently body positive, but it's not
easy to be kick-ass all the time. Especially when someone tells
you point blank to your face that you are fat and you need
to lose weight or you will . . . (insert really scary reason here
usually culminating in the fact that you will be fat, alone, and
unlovable until you lose some weight).*

*And I absolutely guarantee that inside every phenomenal
kick-ass fat positive role model is the tiniest inkling of doubt
and fear, and every once and a while, when you are feeling
a little vulnerable, even the toughest, most awesome girl can
be tripped up, even if they refuse to admit it. I'll even go out
on a limb and say that I believe this wholeheartedly—anyone
who tells you this is lying. This is not to say that we should
just succumb to the cultural standards and get all weak in our
knees when someone calls us fat. We will keep fighting and
loving ourselves no matter what and becoming role models for
other women to follow in our example, BUT there has to be
some room for honesty in the equation. And honestly? It is not
always easy being a Body Image Warrior.*[1]

We have to realize that we learn and internalize that we are not
okay throughout *our entire lives.* For me, that's over a quarter of a cen-
tury's worth of self-hate, indoctrination, and brainwashing. It's going
to take a lot longer than you think to reverse this thinking, and it's
definitely not going to happen overnight. It's not about having 100 percent positive days; that would be unrealistic. It's about working toward
having more good days than bad. Even if it's just one extra confident
day a week . . . that's progress.

Allow yourself to have "weak" days. Cry, mourn, sob, yell, throw
things. Whichever. Then get up, brush yourself off, give the media the
finger, and move forward because you're a fucking warrior, okay?

Okay. So if y'all were to try this shit that I wrote in some book, what would happen? What would be the payoff?

If we were to embrace everything I just typed out for days on end hiding in my room until I ran out of episodes of *Agent Carter* and *Arrow* to watch, my fingers started bleeding, and my cats forgot who I am . . . what's the payoff?

Well, first and foremost, our lives would be awesome. We'd shrug off the ridiculous standards that are made up to hurt us, flip the bird at every billboard, take care of our brains, ask for help, treat our bodies with kindness, take pictures of ourselves, walk without apologizing, eat that motherfucking tiramisu, wear that shirt we love, kiss that person we like, get that job we know we'd be good at, try that new position in bed, teach our kids some kindness, tell ourselves we're amazing every day before we walk out the door . . . y'know. Basic awesome stuff.

And hot damn, that's GOOD ENOUGH FOR ME!

But there's actually more.

See, if you're doing that—and I'M doing that, and HE'S doing that, and SHE'S doing that, and THEY'RE doing that—there's a whole lot of awesome shit going on at the same time. And this is gonna impact our world a little bit. And by a little bit, I mean a shit ton.

If people let GO of this oppressive thought that they're not good enough, that the way they move around in this world isn't good enough . . . I bet big things will change.

I bet we'll see happier days. Happier days and higher self-esteem. I bet we'll see self-induced depression minimized. Mental illnesses will never go away, no . . . but those created as a result of us being told we're inferior will. I bet we'll see increased goal setting. By adults, by kids, by adult kids . . . everyone will have one less barrier to success. We'll see vacations happening! People with thousands of additional dollars and finding better ways to spend them. I bet we'll see productivity increase in all areas; now that we're not so preoccupied with trying to cover up our flaws, we'll have time on our hands! I bet we'll have better communication and excellent relationships. We'll feel lovable and be able to love. We'll be able to communicate with loved ones, friends, family, and coworkers better than ever before. And I have absolutely no research to back this up, but I have a feeling that there would be more sex. If you want it, you'll have it . . . and, dear god, a world full of orgasms is one I DEFINITELY want to live in.

Kindness would ensue. The race toward perfection would end. Equality would find its place. Judgment would decrease. Diversity would be more diverse. Health care would be unbiased. Hiring processes would become fairer. Compassion would make a comeback. Connections would be made. Everyone would get a seat at the motherfucking table.

Okay, fine. I'm a little bit of an idealist.

But real talk: If we were all to embrace the concept of body love—every single one of us—we would be breathing life into our communities on a monumental level, and our world would shift into a more copacetic and compassionate place.

And the cool thing about all this change? It starts with one person at a time.

Me. Her. Him. Them.

And you.

Because your decision to make a life shift toward body love isn't one that can be made by someone else, and even better, it can't be taken *away* by anyone else. It's an internal decision that no one else can touch. It's yours, and if you decide you're okay, guess what? You're okay. If you decide you're beautiful . . . you're beautiful. If you decide you're perfect just the way you are, in fact *you are perfect just the way you are*. And no one can touch that.

We get to look the status quo straight in the eyeballs like a badass bitch and say: I'M NOT BUYING THAT ANYMORE.

We all deserve to have a life that is full, fulfilling, successful, and happy. And that looks different for everyone depending on what they prioritize in life. But let me just tell you this: If you wanna make a shit ton of money, you deserve it. If you want to have a wide circle of really

THE
**FAT
PEOPLE:**
do all the things!
CHALLENGE
*

#12: LIVE.

Everyone deserves to live a creative, purpose-ful, adventurous, successful, love-filled, happy, happy life. Yes, even you. You deserve to take up space. You deserve to fall in love with your body. You deserve to live.

This challenge is both the easiest and the hard-est: Find your favorite form of creativity and fill your life with it. Find your purpose—one that excites and fulfills you. Find adventure; there is no right or wrong way to do this. Find your version of success; define it yourself. Fall in love with yourself, and allow others to love you. Fuck what others say, and live the life you choose.

Go live.

That's my only order.

good friends, you deserve it. If you want a simple and beautiful living space, you deserve it. If you want three cats, you deserve it. If you want to become a slam poet, you deserve it. If you want a tiny apartment just to yourself, you deserve it. If you want a moment to read alone, you deserve it. If you want to start a new group in town to watch clouds, you deserve it! If you want to just exist in peace, you deserve it. YOU, my love, are the creator of your life. Only you. And so decide what it is that you want. Know that you deserve it. And work toward it in what-ever way you decide. Be the motherfucking captain of your own ship.

And I *know* opportunity isn't equal. That life isn't fair, and some-times it's not even remotely kind. I know that sometimes gigantic bar-riers get in the way of that perfect dream we see in our future. But one thing that will never change in this world of ours is the fact that we need and deserve all the happiness, success, love, kindness, and joy we can get our hands on. So don't let your self-doubts stop you; whatever you want . . . you already deserve it.

Now, I have one last thing to tell you, so listen up.

You are fucking beautiful. I'm saying this with a straight face and seriously meaningful look where I maintain eye contact for an uncomfortable amount of time. I know you may not feel like you fit into the category of gorgeous that our world has created. I know that it's hard. I know that it's a daily battle. But fuck their fascist beauty standards. The second you stop looking for someone else in your mirror and start looking at YOU is the second you will start to appreciate what you are. Stop looking for flaws. Stop looking for differences. You are perfect. You are more than enough. You are the best thing that has ever happened to you. And you are fucking beautiful.

Now say it with me.

※

resources

Note: The body positive activism movement is multifaceted in the way that the feminist movement is multifaceted. There are different approaches, schools of thinking, and ways of learning, much like feminism and other movements as well. Of course, while pieces might move independently, body positive activism proponents all believe the same thing. Something akin to: All bodies are equal.

I've created a list of websites, blogs, social media sites, and resources for you that relate to body activism. I'm definitely not responsible for the content on these sites, because, y'know, I have zero control over what they post; as of now, though, I believe these resources may be helpful for you. If you find one that doesn't work for you or you disagree with, don't fret. Skip it and go find the ones that do!

Body Positive Websites

1. 365 Day Project: www.365dayproject.org.au

2. About Face: www.about-face.org

3. The Adipositivity Project: www.adipositivity.com

4. A Beautiful Body Project: www.abeautifulbodyproject.com

5. Association for Size Diversity and Health: www.sizediversity andhealth.org

6. Beauty Redefined: www.beautyredefined.org

7. Be Nourished: benourished.org

8. Be Your Own Beloved: www.viviennemcmasterphotography.com

9. Big Beautiful Wellness: bigbeautifulwellness.com

10. Body Image Movement: bodyimagemovement.com.au

11. The Body Is Not an Apology: thebodyisnotanapology.com

12. The Booty Revolution: thebootyrevolution.tumblr.com

13. Curvy Yoga: www.curvyyoga.com

14. Dr. Deah's Body Shop: www.drdeah.com

15. Everyday Feminism: everydayfeminism.com

16. The Fat Chick: www.thefatchick.com

17. Fat Girl Food Squad: fatgirlfoodsquad.com

18. Fat!So?: www.fatso.com

19. Fierce Freethinking Fatties: fiercefatties.com

20. Flat and Fabulous: www.flatandfabulous.org

21. Health at Every Size: www.haescommunity.org

22. A Healthy Paradigm: ahealthyparadigm.wordpress.com

23. Herself: herself.com

24. Isabel Foxen Duke: isabelfoxenduke.com

25. Junkfood Science: junkfoodscience.blogspot.com

26. Let's Queer Things Up: letsqueerthingsup.com

27. Linda Bacon: www.lindabacon.org

28. Move and Be Free: www.moveandbefree.com

29. Operation Beautiful: www.operationbeautiful.com

30. This Girl Can: www.thisgirlcan.co.uk

31. Women Using Art for Body Acceptance: wuafba.wordpress.com

32. And basically everything written by:
Lesley Kinzel: xojane.com/author/lesley
Marianne Kirby: xojane.com/author/marianne

Facebook Pages Worth Following

1. Beauty Redefined: facebook.com/BeautyRedefined

2. Beauty Is Inside: facebook.com/BeautyIsInside.page

3. Bodies Born to Rise: facebook.com/pages/Bodies-Born-to-Rise

4. The Body Is Not an Apology: facebook.com/The-Body-Is-Not-an-Apology

5. Born to Reign Athletics: facebook.com/borntoreignathletics

6. Curvy and Confident: facebook.com/CurvyAndConfidentFan

7. Curvy Girl Lingerie: facebook.com/CurvyGirlInc

8. Curvy Yoga: facebook.com/curvyyoga

9. Fattitude the Movie: facebook.com/fattitudethemovie

10. Fit Villians: facebook.com/ChichiKix

11. Flat and Fabulous: www.facebook.com/FlatANDFabulous

12. Gala Darling: facebook.com/xogaladarling

13. Linda Bacon: facebook.com/LindaBaconHAES

14. More of Me to Love: facebook.com/moreofmetolove

15. Operation Beautiful: facebook.com/OfficialOperationBeautiful

16. Plus Size Mommy Memoirs: facebook.com/plussizemommymemoirs

17. This Girl Can: facebook.com/pages/This-Girl-Can

18. Tess Holliday: facebook.com/TessHollidayOfficial

19. Blogs

1. Amanda Trusty Says: www.amandatrustysays.com

2. Brittany Herself: brittanyherself.com

3. Chronicles of a Mixed Fat Chick: mixedfatchick.com

4. Curvy Girl Lingerie: curvygirlinc.com

5. Dances with Fat: danceswithfat.wordpress.com/blog

6. Fat Girl, PhD: www.fatgirlphd.com

7. The Fat Nutritionist: www.fatnutritionist.com

8. Feminist Cupcake: feministcupcake.wordpress.com

9. Gala Darling: galadarling.com

10. The Militant Baker: www.themilitantbaker.com

11. Plus Size Birth: plussizebirth.com

12. Plus Size Princess: plussizeprincess.com

13. Tastefully Ratchet: tastefullyratchet.com

14. Virgie Tovar: www.virgietovar.com/blog

15. A Year Without Mirrors: www.ayearwithoutmirrors.com

Body Positive Tumblrs

1. The Adipositivity Project: adipositivityproject.tumblr.com

2. Beautiful Magazine: beautifulmagazine.tumblr.com

3. The Body Love Conference: bodyloveconference.tumblr.com

4. Body Posi: body-posi.tumblr.com

5. Body Positivity for the Modern Man: bodypositivityforthe modernman.tumblr.com

6. Chinese Fashion Lovers: chinesefashionlovers.tumblr.com

7. Chubby Bunny: chubby-bunnies.tumblr.com

8. Chubby Cupcake: chubby-cupcake.tumblr.com

9. Fat Art: fatart.tumblr.com

10. Fat Can Dance: fatcandance.tumblr.com

11. Fat People Art: fatpeopleart.tumblr.com

12. Fat People of Color: fatpeopleofcolor.tumblr.com

13. Fit Villians: fitvillains.tumblr.com

14. Fuck Yeah Body Image; fuckyeahbodyimage.tumblr.com

15. Fuck Yeah Body Positivity: fuckyeahbodypositivity.tumblr.com

16. Fuck Yeah Hard Femme: fuckyeahhardfemme.tumblr.com

17. Fuck Yeah VBO: fyeahvbo.tumblr.com

18. Guatemalan Rebel: guatemalanrebel.tumblr.com

19. Halt the Body Hate: halt-the-body-hate.tumblr.com

20. Hey Fat Chick: heyfatchick.tumblr.com

21. His Black Dress: hisblackdress.tumblr.com

22. Life Outside the Binary: lifeoutsidethebinary.com

23. I Love Fat: ilovefat.tumblr.com

24. Lotsa Lipstick: lotsalipstick.tumblr.com

25. The Love Yourself Challenge: theloveyourselfchallenge.tumblr.com

26. The Militant Baker, obvs: themilitantbaker.tumblr.com

27. Natural Bods: naturalbods.tumblr.com

28. Old Time Fatties: oldtimefatties.tumblr.com

29. Plus Size Belly Dance: plussizebellydance.tumblr.com

30. Queer Bodies Are: queerbodies.tumblr.com

31. Redefining Body Image: redefiningbodyimage.tumblr.com

32. Sex and Body Positive: bodypositivesexpositive.tumblr.com

33.   A Thick Girls Closet: athickgirlscloset.tumblr.com

34.   Thou Shalt Love Thyself: thoushaltlovethyself.tumblr.com

35.   Transgender Revolution: stuffchrissylikes.tumblr.com

36.   Your Life in Design: www.yourlifeindesign.com

Fatshion and Plus-Size Blogs

1. A Curious Fancy: www.curiousfancy.com

2. Amarachi Ukachu: www.amarachiukachu.com

3. And I Get Dressed: www.andigetdressed.com

4. Ashley Rose: www.thisisashleyrose.com

5. Beauticurve: www.beauticurve.com

6. The Big Girl Blog: www.thisisashleyrose.com

7. Big Hips Red Lips: www.bighipsredlips.com

8. Big or Not to Big: www.big-or-not-to-big.com

9. Born in Sequins: www.borninsequins.com

10. Chubble Bubble: www.chubblebubbleblog.blogspot.com

11. Chubstr: www.chubstr.com

12. Cupcake's Clothes: www.cupcakesclothes.com

13. Curves and Chaos: www.curvesandchaos.com

14. Curvy Girl Chic: www.curvygirlchic.com

15. Danimezza: www.danimezza.com

16. Definatalie: www.definatalie.com

17. Dollface: www.dollface-is-candysweet.blogspot.com

18. Dressing Outside the Box: www.dressingoutsidethebox.com

19. Fashion Hayley: www.fashionhayley.com

20. Fat in the City: www.fatinthecity.com

21. Fatshion Insider: www.fatshioninsider.blogspot.com

22. Fat Shopaholic: www.fatshopaholic.com

23. From the Corners of the Curve: www.fromthecornersofthe-curve.com

24. Gabifresh: www.gabifresh.com

25. Garner Style: www.garnerstyle.blogspot.com

26. Hippopotamuslee: www.hippopotamuslee.blogspot.com

27. His Black Dress: www.hisblackdress.tumblr.com

28. In the Thick of It: www.thickofit.com

29. Jay Miranda: www.jaymiranda.com

30. Margie Plus: www.margieplus.com

31. Musings of a Curvy Lady: www.musingsofacurvylady.com

32. Nadia Boulhosn: www.nadiaaboulhosn.com

33. Nicolette Mason: www.nicolettemason.com

34. Pashteit: www.pashteit.blogspot.co.uk

35. P.S. It's Fashion: www.psitsfashion.com

36. Style it Online: www.styleitonline.com

37. Stylish Curves: www.stylishcurves.com

38. The Curvy and Curly Closet: www.thecurvyandcurlycloset.com

39. The Je Ne Sais Quoi: www.thejenesaisquoi.blogspot.com

40. This is Meagan Kerr: www.thisismeagankerr.com

41. Tutus and Tiny Hats: www.tutusandtinyhats.wordpress.com

42. Twee Valley High: www.tweevalleyhigh.com

43. When In Doubt Wear Purple: www.whenindoubtwearpurple.blogspot.com

44. With Wonder and Whimsy: www.withwonderandwhimsy.com

45. Zero Style: www.zerostyleblog.com

Mental Health Resources

TO FIND A PROFESSIONAL:

1. Mental Health Help Hotlines
www.womenshealth.gov/mental-health/hotlines

2. Behavioral Health Treatment Services Locator
www.findtreatment.samhsa.gov

3. Talkspace
www.talkspace.com

HOTLINES:

1. National Hopeline Network (Crisis Hotline)
1-800-SUICIDE // 1-800-784-2433

2. National Suicide Prevention Lifeline
1-800-273-TALK // 1-800-273-8255

3. Suicide and Crisis Hotline and Adolescent Crisis Intervention
and Counseling Nineline
1-800-999-9999

4. Adolescent Suicide Hotline
1-800-621-4000

5. Suicide Prevention—The Trevor HelpLine
(specializing in gay and lesbian youth suicide prevention)
1-800-850-8078

6. Mental Health Crisis Hotline
In crisis? Call: 1-800-273-TALK

7. The Trans* Lifeline
"Dedicated to the wellbeing of transgender people"
US: 877-565-8860
Canada: 877-330-6366

HELP FINDING A THERAPIST
1. 1-800-THERAPIST/1-800-843-7274

MENTAL HEALTH APPS:
There are a variety of mental health–related apps that can assist you wherever you are. ACT Coach, AETAS, DBT Diary Card and Skills Coach, Depression CBT Self-Help Guide, How Are You, MindShift, PTSD Coach, Stress and Anxiety Coach, and Worry Watch are just a few of the options available at the time of print.

For more mobile and web options, check out www.greatist.com/grow/resources-when-you-can-not-afford-therapy

Books to Read:

1. *An Unapologetic Fat Girl's Guide to Exercise*, by Hanne Blank

2. *The Beauty Myth*, by Naomi Wolf

3. *Big Big Love*, by Hanne Blank

4. *Body Respect*, by Linda Bacon, PhD, and Lucy Aphramor, PhD

5. *Cunt*, by Inga Muscio

6. *Fat Girl Finishing School*, by Rachel Wiley

7. *Fat Girl Walking*, by Brittany Gibbons

8. *Fat! So?*, by Marilyn Wann

9. *Health at Every Size*, by Linda Bacon, PhD

10. *Hot and Heavy: Fierce Fat Girls on Life, Love, and Fashion*, edited by Virgie Tovar

11. *Lessons from the Fat-o-sphere*, by Kate Harding and Marianne Kirby

12. *SparkleFat*, by Melissa May

13. *Two Whole Cakes*, by Lesley Kinzel

*

notes

INTRODUCTION

1. Marianne Kirby, "Go On and Call Me Fat; It's True," xoJane, May 30, 2013, www.xojane.com/issues/saying-the-f-word-fat-fat-fat.
2. Holly Hilgenberg, "Better Homes & Bloggers," Bitch no.54, 2012.

CHAPTER 1

1. Lindsay King-Miller, "Pretty Unnecessary," *Bitch*, no. 65, Winter 2015.
2. Sonya Renee Taylor, December 3, 2014, comment on "Pretty Unnecessary," *Bitch Media*, http://bitchmagazine.org/article/pretty-unnecessary-beauty-body-positivity.
3. Dr. Nancy Etcoff, Dr. Susie Orbach, Dr. Jennifer Scott, Heidi D'Agostino, "The Real Truth About Beauty: A Global Report," commissioned by Dove, accessed April 9, 2015, http://www.dove.us/docs/pdf/19_08_10_The_Truth_About_Beauty-White_Paper_2.pdf.
4. National Association of Anorexia Nervosa and Eating Disorders (ANAD), "Eating Disorders Statistics," accessed April 9, 2015, www.anad.org/get-information/about-eating-disorders/eating-disorders-statistics.
5. G. B. Schreiber, M. Robins, R. Striegel-Moore, E. Obarzanek, J. A. Morrison, D. J. Wright, "Weight Modification Efforts Reported by Black and White Preadolescent Girls: National Heart, Lung, and Blood Institute Growth and Health Study," National Center for Biotechnology Information, U.S. National Library of Medicine, National Institutes of Health, July 1996, accessed April 9, 2015, www.ncbi.nlm.nih.gov/pubmed/8668414.
6. ANAD, "Eating Disorders Statistics."
7. Ibid.

CHAPTER 2

1. Toothpaste for Dinner, February 6, 2013, www.toothpastefordinner. com/index.php?date=020613.

2. Brené Brown, *The Gifts of Imperfection: Let Go of Who You Think You're Supposed to Be and Embrace Who You Are* (Center City, Minn.: Hazelden, 2010).

CHAPTER 3

1. Jared Diamond, *Guns, Germs, and Steel: The Fate of Human Societies* (New York: W. W. Norton, 1998), pp. 104–113.

2. Laura Fraser, *Losing It: America's Obsession with Weight and the Industry That Feeds on It* (New York: Dutton, 1997), pp. 16.

3. Ibid.

4. Rothblum, Esther D. *The Fat Studies Reader.* New York: New York University Press, 2009.

5. Naomi Wolf, *The Beauty Myth: How Images of Beauty Are Used Against Women* (New York: W. Morrow, 2002), pp. 58–85.

6. Ibid.

7. Booth, Barbara, "Real Men Don't Cry—but They Are Exfoliating. Say Hello to 'Mampering,'" CNBC. December 6, 2014, www.cnbc. com/id/102241557#.

CHAPTER 4

1. Geoff Williams, "The Heavy Price of Losing Weight," *U.S. News & World Report—Money*, January 2, 2013, http://money.usnews.com/ money/personal-finance/articles/2013/01/02/the-heavy-price-of-losing-weight.

2. American Society of Plastic Surgeons, "2012 Plastic Surgery Statistics Report," http://www.plasticsurgery.org/Documents/news-resources/statistics/2012-Plastic-Surgery-Statistics/full-plastic-surgery-statistics-report.pdf.

3. Beth Greenfield, "Fat Pride Activist Inspires Curvy Girls to Show

Some Skin This Summer," *Yahoo! Health,* August 8, 2014, www. yahoo.com/health/fat-pride-activist-inspires-curvy-girls-to-show-some-94178904482.html.

4. *This American Life,* episode 545, WBEZ Chicago's This American Life episode #545: "If You don't Have Anything Nice to Say, SAY IT IN ALL CAPS." aired January 23, 2015, www.thisamericanlife.org/radio-archives/episode/545/transcript.

5. Comment on Prince Ea, "How to Instantly Defeat Any Hater," December 2014, accessed May 1, 2015, www.youtube.com/watch?v=1wZEP5ZHZpA.

6. Meghan Tonjes, YouTube, www.youtube.com/watch?v=wTmEEZsm3Dk.

7. *This American Life,* "If You Don't Have Anything Nice to Say."

8. Paulo Freire, Pedgogy of the Oppressed, 30th Anniversay Edition (New York: Bloomsbury Academic, 2000).

9. Plus size style blogger Gabi Gregg of Gabifresh

10. Sara C. Nelson, "This Plus Size Model Has a Message for Every Woman Who Ever Doubted Herself," *The Huffington Post UK,* January 26, 2015, www.huffingtonpost.co.uk/2015/01/26/plus-size-model-tess-munster-message-every-woman-doubted-her-self-_n_6546768.html.

10. Kelsey Miller, "The Problem with Fat Monica," *Refinery 29,* December 22, 2014, http://www.refinery29.com/fat-characters-tv-movies#page-1.

GUEST ESSAY: ANDREW WHALEN

1. Matthew B. Feldman and Ilan H. Meyer, "Eating Disorders in Diverse Lesbian, Gay, and Bisexual Populations," *International Journal of Eating Disorders* 40, no. 3 (April 2007): 218–226.

CHAPTER 5

1. Steven Blair, P.E.D., Cooper Institute for Aerobics Research, 1997, www.obesitymyths.com/myth4.1.htm.

2. American Medical Association House of Delegates, "Recognition of Obesity as a Disease," May 16, 2013, www.npr.org/documents/2013/jun/ama-resolution-obesity.pdf; Harriet Brown, "How Obesity Became a Disease," *The Atlantic*, March 24, 2015, www.theatlantic.com/health/archive/2015/03/how-obesity-became-a-disease/388300.

3. T. Mann, A. J. Tomiyama, E. Westling, A. M. Lew, B. Samuels, J. Chatman, "Medicare's Search for Effective Obesity Treatments: Diets are Not the Answer," *American Psychologist* 62 (April 2007), quoted in Kate Harding and Marianne Kirby, *Lessons From the Fat-o-sphere: Quit Dieting and Declare a Truce with Your Body* (New York: Perigee Books, 2009).

4. Ragen Chastain, "Do 95% of Dieters Really Fail?" accessed May 2, 2015, https://danceswithfat.wordpress.com/2011/06/28/do-95-of-dieters-really-fail.

5. Rick Nauert, PhD, "75% of Women Have Disordered Eating," *PsychCentral*, 2008, www.psychcentral.com/news/2008/04/23/75-percent-of-women-have-disordered-eating/2181.html.

6. Gaesser, Glenn A., *Big Fat Lies: The Truth About Your Weight and Your Health* (Carlsbad, Calif.: Gurze Books, 2002).

7. L. Henry, "Even Kids are Suffering from Anorexia and Bulimia," http://eatingdisorders.suite101.com/article.cfm/eating_disorders_in_children. See more at http://www.nursingcenter.com/lnc/cearticle?tid=1031497#P79.

8. G. D. Foster, T. A. Wadden, A. P. Makris, D. Davidson, R. S. Sanderson, D. B. Allison, A. Kessler, "Primary Care Physicians' Attitudes About Obesity and Its Treatment," *Obes Res*, October 2003, 11(10): 1168–7, www.ncbi.nlm.nih.gov/pubmed/14569041.

9. Marlene B. Schwartz, Heather O'Neal Chambliss, Kelly D. Brownell, Steven N. Blair, and Charles Billington, "Weight Bias Among Health Professionals Specializing in Obesity," 2003, www.size-acceptance.org/downloads/weight_bias_among.pdf.

10. Albino Blacksheep Cartoon. www.albinoblacksheep.com/bogswallop

11. Rachel P. Wildman, Paul Muntner, Kristi Reynolds, Aileen P. McGinn, Swapril Rajpathak, Judith Wyle-Rosett, MaryFran R. Sowers, "The Obese Without Cardiometabolic Risk Factor Clustering and the Normal Weight with Cardiometabolic Risk Factor Clustering: Prevalence and Correlates of 2 Phenotypes Among the U.S. Population (NHANES 1999-2004)," *Archives of Internal Medicine*, 2008,168(15): 1617–24.

12. Linda Bacon and Lucy Aphramor, *Body Respect: What Conventional Health Books Get Wrong, Leave Out, and Just Plain Fail to Understand About Weight* (Dallas, Tex.: BenBella Books, 2004).

GUEST ESSAY: JEN MCLELLAN

1. Angelina R. Sutin and Antonio Terracciano (2013), "Perceived Weight Discrimination and Obesity," PLoS ONE 8(7): e70048. doi:10.1371/journal.pone.0070048.

CHAPTER 6

1. Tina Fey, *Bossypants* (New York: Little, Brown and Company, 2011).

2. http://blog.modcloth.com/2014/09/03/fashion-truth-letter/

3. *Oxford Dictionary Online*, "Selfie," accessed May 2, 2015, www.oxforddictionaries.com/definition/english/selfie.

4. "American Society of Plastic Surgeons: 2012 Plastic Surgery Statistics Report 2012," www.plasticsurgery.org/Documents/news-resources/statistics/2012-Plastic-Surgery-Statistics/full-plastic-surgery-statistics-report.pdf.

5. *Mayo Clinic Online*, Diseases and Conditions: Cellulite, accessed May 2, 2015, www.mayoclinic.org/diseases-conditions/cellulite/basics/causes/CON-20029901.

6. Pia Schiavo-Campo, *Chronicles of a Mixed Fat Chick*, http://mixed-fatchick.com. Personal Communication.

7. Naomi Wolf, *The Beauty Myth: How Images of Beauty Are Used Against Women* (New York: W. Morrow, 2002).

8. Carl Haub, "How Many People Have Ever Lived on Earth?" Population Reference Bureau, October 2011. www.prb.org/publications/articles/2002/HowManyPeopleHaveEverLivedonEarth.aspx

9. Runfola, Cristin, et al., 2013, "Characteristics of Women with Body Size Satisfaction at Midlife: Results of the Gender and Body Image (GABI) Study," www.tandfonline.com/doi/abs/10.1080/08952841.2013.816215.

10. Charing Ball, "More Than the Coke Bottle Look: Why Plus-Size Isn't as Diverse as It Should Be," *Madame Noire*, May 28, 2014. www.madamenoire.com/433708/plus-size-isnt-really-diverse.

CHAPTER 7

1. Joshua Brustein, "Americans Now Spend More Time on Facebook Than They Do on Their Pets," *Bloomberg Business*, July 23, 2014, www.bloomberg.com/bw/articles/2014-07-23/heres-how-much-time-people-spend-on-facebook-daily.

2. Lynda G. Boothroyd, Martin J. Tovée, Thomas V. Pollet, "Visual Diet Versus Associative Learning as Mechanisms of Change in Body Size Preferences," *PLOS ONE*, November 7, 2012, journals.plos.org/plosone/article?id=10.1371/journal.pone.0048691.

3. Nancy Shute, "How Changing Visual Cues Can Affect Attitudes About Weight," *NPR*, November 9, 2012, www.npr.org/blogs/health/2012/11/09/164789823/how-changing-visual-cues-can-affect-attitudes-about-weight.

CHAPTER 8

1. National Alliance on Mental Illness, "Mental Illness Facts and Numbers," accessed May 1, 2015, www.nami.org/factsheets/mental-illness_factsheet.pdf.

2. National Institute of Mental Health, "Serious Mental Illness (SMI) Among U.S. Adults," accessed May 1, 2015, www.nimh.nih.gov/ health/statistics/prevalence/serious-mental-illness-smi-among-us-adults.shtml.

3. *Merriam-Webster.com*, "Illness," accessed May 1, 2015, www. merriam-webster.com/dictionary/illness.

4. Susie Campbell, "What If We Treated Every Illness the Way We Treat Mental Illness?" www.themilitantbaker.tumblr.com/ image/117925391428.

CHAPTER 9

1. Naomi Wolf, *The Beauty Myth: How Images of Beauty Are Used Against Women* (New York: W. Morrow, 2002), pp. 14.

2. Bevin Branlandingham, "How to Be a Good Ally to Fat People Who Appear to Have Lost Weight," *Queer Fat Femme*, www. queer-fatfemme.com/2013/10/04/how-to-be-a-good-ally-to-fat-people-who-appear-to-have-lost-weight.

3. Ibid.

4. Virgie Tovar, *Hot & Heavy: Fierce Fat Girls on Life, Love, & Fashion* (Berkeley, Calif.: Seal Press, 2012).

5. Ragen Chastain, "The Underpants Rule and You," *Dances with Fat*, June 6, 2012, www.danceswithfat.wordpress.com/2012/06/06/the-underpants-rule-and-you.

6. "Jessica's Daily Affirmation," YouTube video, 0:50, posted by "dmchatster," June 16, 2009, https://www.youtube.com/ watch?v=qR3rK0kZFkg.

CHAPTER 10

1. Chastity, *GarnerStyle*, "#BoycottingTarget #AltuzarraForTarget," August 14, 2014, *Garnerstyle*, www.garnerstyle.blogspot. com/2014/08/im-boycotting-target-altuzarra-for-target.html.

2. Leeann Duggan, "Why One Woman Is Boycotting Target over the Altuzarra Collab," *Refinery 29*, August 15, 2014, www.refinery29. com/2014/08/72955/boycott-target-movement.

3. Benoit Denizet-Lewis, "The Man Behind Abercrombie & Fitch," January 24, 2006, *Salon.com*. www.salon.com/2006/01/24/jeffries.

4. Matthew Shaer, "Why Abercrombie Is Losing Its Shirt," February 8, 2014, *New York Magazine*, www.nymag.com/thecut/2014/02/why-abercrombie-is-losing-its-shirt.html.

5. ModCloth, "More U.S. Women Report Wearing a Size 16 Dress Than a Size 2 and 0 Combined—ModCloth Introduces Full Range of Sizes," June 14, 2013, http://www.modcloth.com/about_us/press-release--june-14-2013.

6. Christopher Muther, "The Worst Trend for the Summer of 2013? The Dreaded Crop Top," April 10, 2013, *The Boston Globe*. www.boston-globe.com/lifestyle/style/2013/04/10/the-worst-trend-for-summer-the-dreaded-crop-top/7T1XjSxRvwSIUAtTJ5D1DP/story.html.

7. Katie J. M. Baker, "The 5 Kinds of Flesh-Obsessed Articles You Read in the Spring," April 11, 2013, *Jezebel*, www.jezebel.com/the-5-kinds-of-flesh-obsessed-articles-you-read-during-472484638.

8. Virgie Tovar, ed., *Hot & Heavy: Fierce Fat Girls on Life, Love & Fashion* (Berkeley, Calif.: Seal Press, 2012).

CHAPTER 11

1. *Wikipedia*, "Neuroplasticity," last modified May 5, 2015, www. en.wikipedia.org/wiki/Neuroplasticity.

2. MedicineNet.com, "Definition of Neuroplasticity," last editorial review June 14, 2012, www.medicinenet.com/script/main/art. asp?articlekey=40362.

3. Jane Porter, "How to Rewire Your Brain for Greater Happiness," August 27, 2014, *Fast Company*, www.fastcompany.com/3034801/the-future-of-work/how-to-rewire-your-brain-for-greater-happiness.

4. Golda Poretsky, "Why It's Okay to Be Fat," YouTube video, posted by TEDx Mill River, May 19, 2003, https://www.youtube.com/watch?v=73SXX0w4eY8.

CHAPTER 12

1. *Madea Goes to Jail*, Lionsgate, 2009.
2. Stephen Chbosky, *The Perks of Being a Wallflower* (New York: Pocket Books, 1999).
3. Marsha M. Linehan, *DBT Skills Training*
4. Susan I. Buchalter, *Raising Self-Esteem in Adults*

CHAPTER 13

1. Mara Glatzel, MaraGlatzel.com, "Glee: Mercedes + the Bout of Negative Body Image," www.maraglatzel.com/gleeky-mercedes-and-the-bout-of-negative-body-image.

✳

acknowledgments

A big fat hug and thank you to my mom for being an inspirational superhero, my grandmother for being the best sounding board in the world, and my partner for cooking me balanced meals while I wrote this book so I wouldn't develop scurvy. And the sex. Thanks, babe, for the sex; it was a lifesaver. Family and friends, thank you as well for being in my corner; it means more to me than 26 letters allow me to say.

I additionally owe infinite thanks to the dozens of body activists that surround me daily for their strength, perseverance, brilliance, and support. This certainly includes the magical minds that contributed to this book. Without all of these folks, the world wouldn't be as bright or my mission as clear. TEAMWORK FOREVER, Y'ALL.

I would also like to thank the dedicated assholes of the internet, considering the fact that every time I got knocked down I was able to get back up even stronger and more resolved. Thanks guys!

And lastly, I'm sending thanks to you, person reading this. I honestly do this type of work because of you. Your support, stories, and stunning survival in this world are what inspire me the most. You're rad. Never forget it, okay?

about the author

Jes Baker is a positive, progressive, and magnificently irreverent force to be reckoned with in the realm of self-love advocacy and mental health.

Jes is internationally recognized for her writing on her blog, The Militant Baker, and for the "Attractive and Fat" campaign, a response to Abercrombie and Fitch's controversial branding efforts. Her extensive body advocacy work has continued to garner attention from hundreds of national and international media networks.

Liora K

When not blogging, Jes spends her time speaking at universities, taking pictures in her underwear, writing for online publications, working with clothing companies to promote more plus-size fashion, and trying to convince her cats that they like to wear sweaters and bow ties.